KNACK
MAKE IT EASY

CALORIE COUNTER
COOKBOOK

KNACK®

CALORIE COUNTER
COOKBOOK

A Step-by-Step Guide to a Delicious, Calorie Conscious Diet

CHANTAL MARTINEAU

Nutritional analysis by Jean Kostak, M.S., R.D., C.D.E.
Photographs by Jackie Alpers

Guilford, Connecticut
An imprint of Globe Pequot Press

Editor in Chief: Maureen Graney
Editor: Katie Benoit
Cover Design: Paul Beatrice, Bret Kerr
Text Design: Paul Beatrice
Layout: Melissa Evarts
Cover photos by Jackie Alpers
All interior photos by Jackie Alpers

Library of Congress Cataloging-in-Publication Data is available on file.

ISBN 978-1-59921-862-5

Printed in China

10 9 8 7 6 5 4 3 2 1

Dedication

For Florence and Rita.

Acknowledgments

Putting together a book like this one requires the communal efforts of a select group of dedicated people. I'd like to thank my editor, Keith Wallman, and Globe Pequot's development editor, Katie Benoit, for guiding me through the process, as well as photographer Jackie Alpers for making my recipes come to life with her beautiful, vivid images, and to nutritionist Jean Kostak for her priceless input. Thank you to my mom, Brenda, for teaching me how to cook so many years ago, and to my dad, Claude, who still makes the meanest breakfast around. And a special thanks to my friends Carolyn, Melissa, and Alix, who shared their ideas and kitchens with me, and to Amy, Sheri, Chic, Wendy, Jennie, Steve, and Gareth, for their love and support through the seemingly endless days of cooking and writing.

—Chantal Martineau

Photographer Acknowledgments

There was so much that happened behind the scenes in producing the images for this book. I would like to thank everyone involved including: Keith Wallman, my editor at Globe Pequot who suggested me for this project; Katie Benoit, Globe Pequot's development editor who has an amazing ability to keep this and so many other projects running smoothly while exuding a calm, positive presence; and Chantal Martineau for coming up with some super tasty and easy-to-prepare recipes for this book—it was truly a pleasure to cook and photograph each of them. Thank you to my husband, Jason, for his love, creative insight, and support, and a special thanks to my two wonderful cats, Zoe and Nova, for keeping me company in the kitchen during long days of shooting.

—Jackie Alpers

CONTENTS

INTRODUCTION

We've all, at one time or another in our lives, tried to lose weight. And most of us have attempted to achieve weight loss through any number of fad diets, crash diets, and get-thin-quick schemes. But the fact is that none of these ultimately works because there is no trick or secret to losing weight or maintaining a healthy weight. A person's weight is determined by the number of calories he or she consumes versus the number of calories he or she expends: calories in, calories out. Keeping track of what you eat, as well as how much you exercise throughout the day, is really the only way to manage your weight.

This book is designed to help teach you how to keep track of what you put into your body, so that you can better understand how to lose weight or maintain your weight. In addition to learning how to portion your meals, you'll learn how to cut the fat in your everyday recipes and how to get the most nutrients possible out of your daily meals and snacks.

Whoever came up with the idea that starving yourself or skipping meals is the way to lose a few pounds had no idea how the body works. When you deny your body food, it immediately goes into survival mode, which means it starts storing fat. Normally, when you eat, your metabolism speeds up. When you skip a meal, your metabolism takes a nosedive, which means you expend less energy. Any weight loss experienced during this time is usually a result of losing water, which you already know your body needs plenty of to survive. With the help of this book, you'll learn how to eat to lose weight or maintain your weight without cutting corners. And you'll have a delicious time doing so!

What's the Deal with Calories, Anyway?

In this book, you'll learn what a calorie is, how many are in the foods you like to eat every day, and how many you should be consuming at each meal. A section containing

journal can help you not only know where most of your calories are coming from, but also can help you to detect where you can trim calories.

An important aspect of keeping track of what you eat is being aware of what you're putting into your body. Whether you're trying to lose weight or simply to maintain a healthy body weight, it's important to get into the habit of reading labels to know exactly what is in the food you eat, as well as how much you should be eating in one sitting. Serving sizes are clearly listed on the labels of all packaged foods.

Giving Your Body What It Needs

Of course, when trying to lose weight or maintain your weight, you risk cutting out important nutrients. Sometimes we become so focused on the caloric value of what we're eating that we forget to take into consideration the nutritional value of foods. People who diet tend to not eat enough vital nutrients, including fiber, calcium, and iron. To counter this, many of the recipes in this book incorporate nutrient-rich foods: fresh fruits and vegetables, beans and nuts, and whole grains like brown rice.

This book aims to focus less on "low-cal" foods and more on healthy and nutritious real foods. For example, instead of

resources, including Web sites, books, and even smart phone applications to help you track calories, can be found at the end of the book.

Why keep track of calories, you ask? Can it really make a difference to know exactly what you've eaten over the course of a day? The answer is yes. Studies have shown that people who write down what they eat are more likely to maintain a healthy weight or achieve weight loss. Keeping a food journal involves writing down everything you've eaten, including all meals and snacks. And don't forget drinks juices, sodas, and alcohol all contain a significant number of calories. Keeping track of all this information in your food

using low-fat cooking sprays, we suggest pouring various heart-healthy oils—olive, avocado, and vegetable—into spray bottles to use when pan-frying or dressing a salad. And instead of calling for, say, lower-fat cream to make sauces or as a baking ingredient, we make use of nonfat yogurt and, in particular, Greek-style yogurt, which is thick and creamy.

In many of the recipes in this book, you might be surprised to find ingredients that contain a significant amount of fat, such as olive oil, nuts, and even avocado. But what this book will try to communicate is the difference between "good" and "bad" fats and how the former are an essential part of a balanced diet. Eating good fats, such as monounsaturated fats, can reverse the negative effects of eating bad fats. Good fats also impart a slew of other health benefits and can help to guard against serious chronic diseases.

Working Out Is Part of the Equation

One of the subjects this book only touches on is exercise. The second half of the calories in, calories out equation is just as important as the first. There are a number of resources, many of which are listed at the end of this book, to help you calculate how many calories your daily activities expend. In addition to going to the gym or to your yoga class, every single activity you undertake burns calories. Whether it's vacuuming the house, sleeping, or walking to work, you cannot help but burn the calories you've eaten throughout the day. To lose weight, you must simply expend more calories than you consume. To lose one pound, you have to burn off 3,500 extra calories. Of course, this shouldn't be done in one day. Weight loss should be undertaken as a gradual process, one that is achieved over time and as a result of a lifestyle change. As we stated at the very beginning of this chapter, crash diets are never the answer.

A healthy, nutritious, calorie-controlled diet combined with regular exercise is the answer. This book briefly explores the different types of exercise you might undertake and which are most beneficial to someone trying to lose weight.

While experts continue to disagree over whether cardio or weight training ultimately burns more calories, it's clear that a combination of the two types of exercise is the best way to lose weight or maintain your weight. Some forms of exercise, such as yoga (depending on the style), incorporate elements of both cardio and strength training.

Finally, this book offers important information about that one thing that can undo any diet: snacking. Often deemed the downfall of anyone trying to lose weight or maintain a healthy weight, snacking can be done in a healthy way and actually help you achieve your weight goals. As stated earlier, allowing your body to become hungry is dangerous. By keeping nutritious real foods on hand to snack on, you can ensure that you won't be reaching for the candy machine when the munchies arise.

The key to maintaining a healthy diet is to keep it simple and eat the foods that you enjoy. This book features super-easy, tasty recipes for dishes that are satisfying and nutritious. The sections are broken up by different caloric values that you can pick and choose from to arrive at the number of calories you wish to take in each day. (Women trying to lose weight should be aiming for 1,400–1,600 calories per day, while men should consume up to 1,800 calories per day.) You're encouraged to mix and match breakfasts, lunches, dinners, and snacks for every day of the week.

CALORIES IN; CALORIES OUT

The equation is easy: the calories you eat minus the calories you burn off through exercise

We know we're supposed to watch our calories. But what are they exactly? Calories are units of food energy. In other words, they're units used to measure how much energy a certain food item contains or a particular physical activity expends.

Everything you eat and do has a caloric value, from the sandwich you just ate to the stick of gum you chewed afterward,

from the yoga class you took to the hour you spent vacuuming the house.

When it comes to weight control, experts affirm that calories are far more important to monitor than fat intake. To lose one pound, a person must burn an average of 3,500 calories more than he or she consumes.

Staying Active Is Key

- Every activity has a caloric value, and this value varies depending on the shape and size of the person doing the activity.

- Jogging one mile burns an average of 100 calories.

- Most yoga classes burn about 200 calories per hour. Cleaning the house can burn up to 250 calories per hour.

- Even chewing burns calories.

Tracking What You Eat

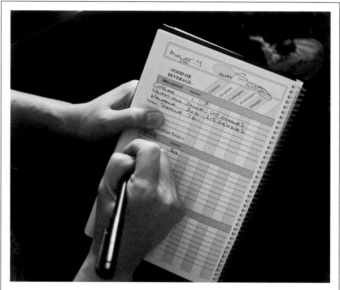

- Studies show that keeping track of what you eat encourages weight loss.

- Keep a food journal that lists your meals and snacks for each day.

- Alternatively, try one of the many online calorie counters. Some also exist in mobile formats for your smart phone.

For women, a healthy body weight can be maintained by eating between 1,400 and 1,600 calories per day. For men, it's closer to 1,600 to 1,800 calories per day. Of course, people who lead very active lifestyles must consume more calories in order to have enough energy to carry out the physical activities they enjoy. Because very active people burn many calories, they are able to maintain a healthy weight. In contrast, people with more sedentary lifestyles have to be careful about consuming too many calories.

ZOOM

To calculate your caloric intake, just do the math: Subtract the calories you burn through your daily exercise and activities from the calories you accumulate from your meals and snacks. If you've eaten 2,000 calories in one day, you should burn at least 2,000 to maintain a healthy weight.

Working Out

- Every type of exercise has a caloric value.

- The debate over which types of exercise burn more calories is a hard one to settle.

- When it comes to weight training versus cardio, cardio burns more calories while you're actually doing it.

Strength Training

- On its own, cardio burns more calories than weight training.

- However, weight training builds more muscle, which allows you to burn more calories when you're not exercising.

- Your body keeps burning calories once you're done with your weight-training workout.

- If weight loss is your goal, a combination of weight training and cardio is ideal.

PORTION CONTROL

What your plate looks like is just as important as what's on it

Trying to lose weight or maintain your weight by denying yourself the foods you love is a difficult way to go about it. Most nutritionists will tell you that, within reason, you can eat what you like, as long as you control how much of it you eat in one sitting. For example, you may like to indulge in chocolate. Well, if you limit yourself to half a bar of good dark chocolate, you're taking in 160 calories, which is a reasonable amount for a snack or dessert. If you love fries, you can let

yourself have a small side dish of baked fries for 140 calories.

In other words, it's less about denying yourself, and more about not overdoing it on your favorite foods. What your plate looks like when you fill it for a meal can help you judge whether you're eating the right amount of the different food items that make up your meals. The "plate method," commonly used by registered nutritionists, is a way to split up your plate so that you get the right amount of protein,

One Portion of Protein

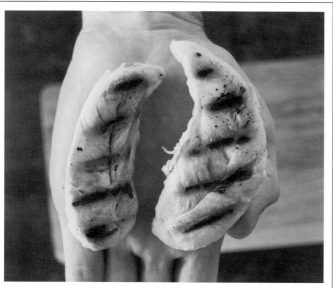

- You don't have to measure every portion down to the milligram. Just eyeball it.
- For one portion of protein—be it chicken, beef, or fish—serve yourself a piece that's about the size of your flattened palm.

One Portion of Good Carbs

- For a portion of good carbs—whole grains like rice, corn, or oatmeal—serve yourself a portion the size of your closed fist.
- A closed fist is about the equivalent of 1 cup of grains or some other carbohydrate, such as potatoes.

vegetables, and starch. Half your plate should be taken up by non-starchy vegetables, such as green beans, salad greens, or broccoli, while the other half should be split between protein, such as chicken, beef, fish, or eggs, and starches like bread, potatoes, rice, or beans.

Of course, you may not be able to have every meal be this balanced, but you can balance your overall daily intake of food. For example, if you have a protein-heavy breakfast like an omelet, have a vegetable-heavy lunch, like a salad. Or if you started your day with carb-filled crepes, you might have chicken soup for lunch and make sure to have a snack of carrot sticks and a low-fat dip. It's not just about taking in the right number of calories, but also about getting all the different kinds of nutrients your body needs to stay healthy.

Whole Grains = Good Carbs

- Good carbs tend to be high in fiber and filling.

- In addition to whole cereal grains, other foods that are considered good carbs include various beans, fruits like apples and oranges, and nuts.

Eyeballing Your Measures

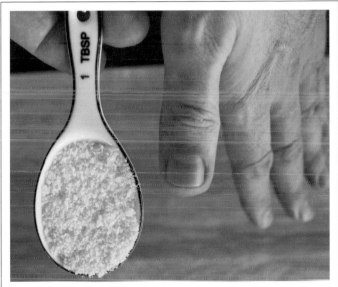

- Does your recipe call for a tablespoon of something? No need to break out the measuring spoons. Just use an amount equal to the size of your thumb.

- For a teaspoon, use an amount equal to the size of the tip of your pinky finger.

- For a dash, use an amount that would fit into the crescent of your pinky nail.

GOOD FAT/BAD FAT

Fats are part of a balanced diet, so long as you know good from bad

For a lot of people who are trying to lose weight or maintain their weight, "fat" can be a four-letter word. The truth is that fats are an important part of our diet. They help the body absorb the nutrients we feed it. The key is to differentiate good fats from bad fats and to maximize intake of the former while minimizing intake of the latter.

You've surely heard of all the different types of fats, but you might not know what each of them really is. Bad fats include saturated fats and trans fats. Saturated fats raise LDL, or "bad cholesterol," levels. They can be found in meats, seafood, dairy products, and certain oils, such as coconut oil. Trans fats, the health effects of which have been hotly debated in recent years, are partially hydrogenated oils (vegetable oils that have had hydrogen added to them through an industrial process to make them more solid). These are often found in processed foods.

Good Fats

- Foods that are high in good fats include olive oil, nuts, avocados, and fish such as tuna and salmon.

- Other oils that are made up largely of good fats include grapeseed oil, flaxseed oil, and canola oil.

Bad Fats

- Foods that are high in bad fats include certain dairy products and many processed snack foods, as well as foods that have been fried.

- Certain oils contain bad fats, including corn oil, palm oil, and coconut oil.

Good fats include monounsaturated and polyunsaturated fats. Monounsaturated fats are generally considered the best kind, as they help maintain HDL, or "good cholesterol," levels, while lowering LDL. Foods that contain mostly monounsaturated fats include olive oil, avocados, some nuts, lard, and duck fat. Polyunsaturated fats also lower LDL cholesterol, but are less stable than the monounsaturated kind when cooked. Soy, corn, sunflower seeds, and fish are high in polyunsaturated fats. Omega-3 fatty acids, which are considered essential to our health, fall into this category. They play an important role in brain function (so, yes, fish *is* brain food!) and have been shown to reduce inflammation and help prevent such chronic illnesses as heart disease, cancer, and arthritis.

It's important to be aware that most foods contain both saturated and unsaturated fats. Good fats can counterbalance the effects of bad fats, but in most cases you can't have one without having the other.

Skinless Chicken

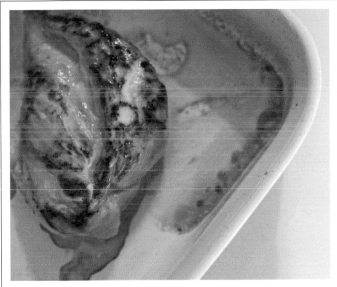

- Trim the fat from certain meats by removing the skin and, literally, the fat.

- For chicken, remove the skin and use the white meat, such as the breast.

- You can also use a combination of white and dark meat for dishes that require a little more flavor.

Fat Trimmed off Meat

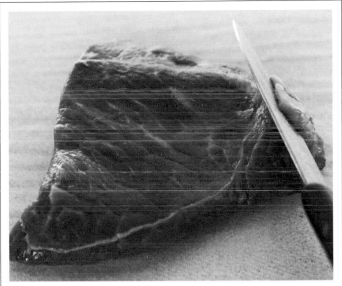

- When preparing beef or pork, choose a cut that is not too marbled and mostly lean.

- If the meat is fatty around the edges, simply trim the fatty part off and use the leaner part of the cut.

FIBER & OTHER NUTRIENTS

Most of us don't eat enough fiber, so make sure you're getting your daily dose

Dieting can lead people to cut certain foods out of their diets. In some cases, this can be a good thing, such as cutting out fried or processed foods. However, eliminating other foods can lead to excluding certain important nutrients that the body needs.

Fiber is one of the most important nutrients to our digestive health, and it is also one of the nutrients most of us don't get enough of. Fiber, also referred to as roughage, is the indigestible part of plant food that helps keep our elimination system intact. It can be found in whole grains, beans and legumes, and certain fruits and vegetables, as well as in nuts and seeds.

Fiber-rich Whole Grains

- Whole grains, such as brown rice, whole wheat bread, barley, and even popcorn, are high in fiber.
- Beans and legumes, such as kidney beans, lima beans, chickpeas, and lentils, are also good sources of fiber.

Fiber-rich Fruit and Veg

- Fruits that are high in fiber include berries, apples, and oranges, as well as dried fruits like dates and prunes.
- Vegetables high in fiber include most dark, leafy greens.

Other nutrients that we sometimes don't get enough of, especially when we're trying to lose weight or maintain our weight, include calcium and iron. Calcium is important not only for healthy bones and teeth, but also for a healthy heart and digestive system. In addition to milk, yogurt, leafy greens, certain beans, and sardines are all excellent sources of calcium.

Iron is a mineral crucial to the health of our circulatory system and can be found in seafood, liver, beef, beans, and pumpkin seeds.

ZOOM

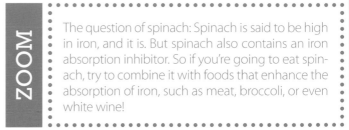

The question of spinach: Spinach is said to be high in iron, and it is. But spinach also contains an iron absorption inhibitor. So if you're going to eat spinach, try to combine it with foods that enhance the absorption of iron, such as meat, broccoli, or even white wine!

High-calcium Foods

- Of course, milk, yogurt, and other low-fat dairy products are good sources of calcium.

- But did you know that rhubarb, sardines, collard greens, almonds, and brussels sprouts are all also great sources of calcium?

Foods High in Iron

- Iron-rich foods include shrimp, lentils, spinach, and blackstrap molasses.

READING LABELS

Take the time to read labels so you can make informed food decisions

Nearly every packaged food sold now must have a label on it outlining the nutritional facts about what's inside. The Nutrition Facts information tells you how much fat, cholesterol, sodium, carbohydrates, protein, vitamins, and minerals are in an average serving of that food.

The first thing to note when reading these labels is the serving size. Some foods, for example, may appear to be packaged in a single serving size, but actually contain more than one "serving." Playing with the serving size allows companies to make misleading claims about how much fat or how many calories a food item contains. If a package of food contains 2.5 servings and you eat the whole thing, you've

Watching Serving Size

- The serving size is calculated according to the typical amount a person would eat as one portion.

- Serving size information is important, as many individual-size food items contain more than one serving.

Daily Value of Nutrients

- The Daily Value of nutrients is usually based on a 2,000- or 2,500-calorie-per-day diet.

- For those of us trying to lose weight or maintain our weight, the figure must be recalculated for a 1,400- or 1,800-calorie per-day diet.

- To do the math, divide the number of calories you're consuming per day by 2,000 or 2,500, then multiply this by the Daily Value amount given to get the right Daily Value for a particular nutrient.

eaten two-and-a-half times the amount recommended and consumed two-and-a-half times the calories, fat, protein, carbs, sodium, etc. indicated on the label.

The nutritional information is also designed to tell you how much of the recommended daily intake of vitamins and minerals a food item contains. The label's information is usually calculated for a 2,000- or 2,500-calorie-per-day diet. If you are on a 1,600- or 1,800-calorie-per-day diet, you will have to adjust the Daily Value information by aiming to consume 80–90 percent of the Daily Value figure given.

The label also lists the ingredients in order of how much is contained in the product. Of course, many ingredients in packaged processed foods are long words that are unfamiliar to us. Some are simply technical terms for ingredients we know, while others are compounds created using industrial processes. Be sure to avoid foods that contain "partially hydrogenated oils," which are trans fat, an industrially processed fat and the worst kind of fat you can eat.

Avoiding Trans Fats

- The Nutrition Information label will tell you if the food item in question contains the wrong kind of fat.

- Partially hydrogenated oils are trans fats, the worst kind of fat to consume, as they raise LDL cholesterol levels and clog arteries.

- Saturated fats should also be avoided. Like trans fats, these can also negatively impact "bad" cholesterol levels.

Check the Ingredients

- The ingredients are listed in the order of the largest amount contained to the smallest amount.

- Food manufacturers sometimes try to hide certain ingredients, such as sugars, which can be listed as fructose, sucrose, and dextrose.

- To avoid MSG, look for terms such as gelatin, yeast extract, and sodium caseinate.

OLIVE OIL

Replace butter and fatty oils with better oils, such as olive

Oil is an integral ingredient in many a delicious recipe. We tend to think of oil as being a fatty substance, which it is, but certain types of oil are better than others. Olive oil, for example, boasts a slew of health benefits in addition to a strong herbal and citrusy flavor.

For the purposes of this book, "olive oil" will refer to extra-virgin olive oil, a staple of Mediterranean cooking. Olive oil is rich in monounsaturated fat, which not only helps boost "good" cholesterol, but also helps lower the bad kind. Cooking with olive oil has been shown to lower your risk of heart disease. Rich in antioxidants, olive oil also has anti-inflammatory properties, which have been linked to lower risk of asthma and rheumatoid arthritis.

Cooking with olive oil instead of butter or other saturated fat–packed oils can significantly boost the nutritional value of a dish. You may have heard that heating olive oil can burn

Butter Label

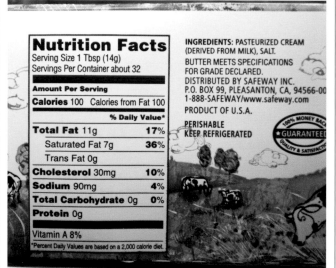

- Cooking with butter can be tasty, but it loads up your dish with saturated fat.

- An ounce of butter has 201 calories, almost all of which are from fat.

- An ounce of butter also accounts for 35 percent of your recommended daily intake of fat. Nearly half of that fat is saturated.

Using Olive Oil

- Replacing butter with olive oil not only boosts the nutritional value of the foods you cook, but also adds a tangy Mediterranean-style flavor.

- It's not just for cooking. Instead of butter, put out a small dish of olive oil (with a splash of balsamic vinegar in it) when you serve bread with a meal.

- For salads and to lubricate pans for frying or sautéing, use olive oil in a pump. Usually, a few sprays are all you need.

off some of the nutrients. The truth is that heating it up can damage its delicate flavors and aromas, but it won't alter the nutrients unless the oil is heated repeatedly, in which case it may slightly oxidize and hydrogenate. Being rich in monounsaturated fats, however, olive oil is highly resistant to these phenomena.

The most delicious and high-quality olive oil is cold pressed. Olive is the only vegetable oil that can be consumed freshly pressed from the original fruit.

ZOOM

E-V-O-Oh? What is the difference exactly between virgin, extra-virgin, and other olive oils? Extra-virgin olive oil is the oil that comes from the first pressing of the olives. It's the purest, highest quality, and best-tasting available. Virgin olive oil is from the second pressing and is less desirable for light cooking or drizzling. Pure olive oil is slightly processed and should only be used for techniques like frying. "Light" olive oil is highly processed with less flavor.

Olive Oil Label

Nutrition Facts
Serving Size 1 tbsp (15 mL)
Servings Per Container about 33

Amount Per Serving

Calories 120	Fat Cal. 120

	% Daily Value*
Total Fat 14g	22%
Saturated Fat 2g	9%
Trans Fat 0g	
Polyunsaturated Fat 2g	
Monounsaturated Fat 10g	
Cholesterol 0mg	0%
Sodium 0mg	0%
Total Carbohydrate 0g	0%
Protein 0g	

Not a significant source of dietary fiber, sugars, vitamin A, vitamin C, calcium and iron.

*Percent Daily Values are based on a 2,000 calorie diet.

DISTRIBUTED BY SAFEWAY INC.
P.O. BOX 99, PLEASANTON, CA 94566-0009
PACKED IN ITALY
OLIVE OIL IS A CHOLESTEROL FREE FOOD.

E.V. OLIVE OIL FROM IT ES TN

SAFEWAY
SELECT.

Extra Virgi
OLIVE OIL

Rich in Flavor

- Compared to butter, olive oil may not appear less fatty at first. An ounce of olive oil has 248 calories and 43 percent of your recommended daily intake of fat. But only 14 percent of that is saturated.

- The unsaturated fats of olive oil help to combat the effects of the saturated fats.

Other Oils

- Olive oil is good for you, but variety is the spice of life.

- Other oils to explore include avocado oil, which is high in antioxidants and boasts a milder, sweeter flavor than olive oil, as well as a higher smoke point (The smoke point refers to the temperature at which

the oil starts to break down, which causes not only smoke, but can undermine the flavor and nutritional value of the oil.)

- Grapeseed oil is also high in antioxidants, and it won't cloud up when chilled the way olive oil does.

DRIED SPICES

Add a pinch of spice to your dish for added flavor and nutrients

When seasoning a dish, many of us add salt and pepper. But adding other dried spices can not only kick up the flavors in your dish, but it can also boost the nutritional value of your food.

There are hundreds of varieties of spices used in cooking around the world. And many of these are available in your average supermarket.

Unfortunately, many of us cook with stale spices that were purchased months or even years ago. When buying dried spices, opt for buying them whole rather than already ground, as the flavors and aromas of the spices last longer in their whole form. For example, a small bottle of ground cinnamon lasts only about three months before becoming stale. But whole cinnamon sticks will still taste fresh upon grinding after well over a year of storage.

Adding a teaspoon or so of dried spice to a dish does very

Paprika

- Paprika comes in mild, sweet, hot, and even smoked varieties.

- In addition to being high in vitamin C, the spice has been shown to improve circulation and help normalize blood pressure.

Turmeric

- Turmeric not only adds a distinctive aromatic dimension to a dish, but it also contributes a golden hue.

- It's a natural antiseptic, and it has been shown to prevent cancer in several studies.

- Turmeric is also a natural anti-inflammatory.

little to affect its caloric value, but can significantly boost its nutritional value. Many spices that have long been used in traditional medicine have now been shown to have scientifically proven medical benefits. Paprika, for example, which is made from dried bell peppers, is high in vitamin C—about nine times higher than tomatoes, largely because of the concentrating effects of drying the peppers in the sun. Vitamin C is an important antioxidant for the health of our immune systems.

Dried cumin, which comes from the seeds of a flowering herb in the parsley family, is not only soothing to the digestive system, but also has been shown to lower the risk of certain types of cancer. The spice, which can be found in Mexican, Indian, and Middle Eastern cooking, also packs a concentrated punch of iron, a mineral that is key to boosting energy and metabolism.

Cumin

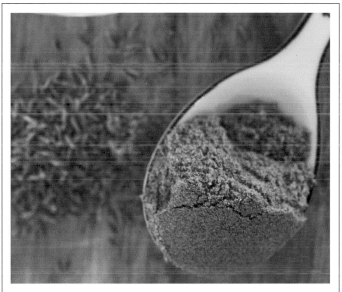

- Cumin has long been used to promote digestion. Adding it to food ensures that you'll get the most from the other nutrients in the dish.

- Oddly, the spice is both a stimulant and a relaxant at once.

- Studies have shown that it can help fight insomnia.

Cinnamon

- Cinnamon can be used in both savory and sweet dishes. High in calcium, fiber, and iron, it has been shown to help prevent certain cancers.

- Antibacterial properties make it a natural preservative for foods.

- Cinnamon also has an anti-clotting effect on the blood.

FRESH HERBS

Be generous when adding fresh herbs to foods—they add color, taste, and nutrients

When you can use fresh herbs in the kitchen, do so. In addition to the nutrients they pack, they can add a healthy dose of color and flavor to a dish.

When cooking with herbs, it's important to know how to prepare them, how much to use, and how to add them to your food. The first thing to keep in mind is to be generous.

Fresh herbs usually require much larger doses than dried spices, as they haven't been concentrated in the drying process.

Delicate herbs, such as basil, parsley, chives, and dill, should be added near the end of cooking so as not to burn off too much of their flavor. Heartier herbs, such as thyme, oregano,

Fresh Parsley

- Parsley is the most popular herb in the world.

- More than just a garnish, it's also one of the most potent disease-fighting herbs on the planet.

- High in iron and vitamin C, it can help fight anemia.

- It's also an excellent source of folic acid, which is crucial to cardiovascular health.

Fresh Basil

- A staple of Italian cooking, fresh basil adds a peppery flavor to any dish.

- It has natural antibacterial properties, as well as anti-inflammatory effects.

and rosemary, can be added earlier on in the preparation of dishes, as the heat from cooking will help spread their flavors throughout the dish.

To prep fresh herbs, make sure they are clean. Soak them in water to remove dirt or soil, then shake or pat dry. Then, remove the leaves from the stems by hand. In the case of leafier herbs, use a sharp chef's knife to chop up the leaves finely. In the case of shrublike herbs, simply add them whole to your dish.

Buying fresh herbs can often mean buying too much, and leftovers won't last long in the crisper. Remedy this by freezing your leftover herbs. Freeze them whole, or make a slurry by tossing them in the blender with a little water, then freeze the slurry in an ice cube tray for easy access.

Another good way of only having what you need on hand is to grow your own herbs. If you don't have a garden, use a window box. Herbs need plenty of sun and little water.

Fresh Mint

- Whether added to sweet or savory dishes or made into a tea, mint can be soothing and refreshing.

- Often used to settle the stomach, mint can also help ease headaches.

- The herb has been shown to help prevent certain cancers.

Fresh Rosemary

- This strongly flavored herb is best used in soups, stews, and meat dishes.

- Studies have shown that it can improve liver function and act as a mild diuretic.

- Rosemary is also good for the skin ... and who doesn't want that?

SNACK FOODS

What you eat between meals can make or break a low-calorie diet

You've probably heard people say that snacking in between meals can be the undoing of any diet. If you're munching on high-fat, high-sodium processed foods full of empty calories, this certainly can be the case. However, eating small meals interspersed with healthful snacks throughout the day has been shown to help with weight management. The idea is to eat when the body is hungry, not when the mind is ravenous, which can lead to consuming much more than is needed.

Stocking your pantry with tasty nibbles, like nuts, dried fruits, and even popcorn, which qualifies as a whole grain, can mean having plenty of nutritious and delicious foods on hand when you get a case of the munchies. After all, most bad food decisions are made in times of intense hunger and as a result of poor planning. So, don't only stock your pantry, but also remember to take snacks with you to work and even when you go out for an afternoon of shopping.

Popcorn

- Few of us think of popcorn as health food. But you can air-pop it or pop it over a stovetop with a little oil for a low-cal snack.

- Instead of using butter and salt, season the popcorn with dried spices or just a little sea salt.

- Air-popped popcorn is a good source of fiber with few calories.

Nuts

- Nuts are high in fat—good fats, mind you, but fat all the same. So it's important to eat them in small quantities.

- Toss them in a trail mix with dried fruit, seeds, and a few semisweet chocolate chips for a satisfying fiber-packed snack.

Instead of relying solely on processed foods labeled "low-cal" or "low-fat," get into the habit of having real foods in the house. A handful of nuts is not only packed with essential heart-healthy oils, but also can easily be combined with some dried fruit and seeds for a quick and satisfying trail mix.

Of course, you'll want to make sure you have fresh fruit and vegetables on hand, especially those that can be consumed raw—maybe dipped in a simple nonfat yogurt–based dip.

Popcorn might be covered in butter and salt at the movie theater, but at home you can top it with a few light seasonings for an easy whole grain snack.

If you do decide to buy processed snack foods, such as tortilla chips for salsa or guacamole, look for the baked versions of popular brands.

Dried Fruit

- Dried fruit has all of the nutrients and sugar of fresh fruit but in a highly concentrated form.

- Sprinkle dried fruit onto a small salad or into yogurt to add fiber and other nutrients to your snack.

- Because it has a long shelf life, dried fruit makes for a great way to enjoy certain fruits out of season.

Baked Corn Chips

- Processed and packaged snacks can be the downfall of any diet. But certain snacks are better for you than others.

- Read the labels on your snack foods to make sure they don't contain partially hydrogenated oils.

- Many snack food makers now produce baked versions of products that were originally fried, such as baked corn and potato chips.

CHOCOLATE . . . YES, CHOCOLATE!

You need not deprive yourself of sweets like chocolate—just buy better chocolate

For many of us, chocolate is a weakness. But it doesn't have to be. Dark or semisweet chocolate is packed with antioxidants and, in small portions, can easily satisfy a craving for something sweet.

Chocolate comes from the cocoa plant and so boasts many of the nutrients found in other dark-colored plants. Studies have shown that eating it can help reduce blood pressure and lower cholesterol levels.

One of the most obvious benefits of chocolate is that it makes us happy. Literally: Eating it releases endorphins, which make us feel euphoric.

If you're going to keep chocolate in the pantry, opt for good

Chocolate Syrup

- Did you know that Hershey's chocolate syrup is fat free?

- Add it to milk or on top of low-fat frozen yogurt for a sinful snack without the guilt.

- You can also try drizzling it over a bowl of sliced strawberries or bananas.

One Portion of Chocolate

- Half of a small organic dark chocolate bar is equal to one portion, around 1 ounce-worth.

- Break up the chocolate and let each square melt on your tongue. (Yes, taking the time to enjoy your chocolate will allow you to be satisfied with less of it!)

- Or layer chocolate on a low-fat tea biscuit for a makeshift chocolate cookie.

quality organic dark chocolate. Half a bar—or 1 ounce—accounts for 160 calories. Pay attention to the cocoa content of the bar. You want your chocolate to be at least 60 percent cocoa. Avoid milk chocolate or white chocolate, as these both have added butter fats.

Of course, chocolate is still high in fat and should be consumed in small quantities, more as a way to add a touch of sweetness to a snack than as a snack on its own. Drizzle a fat-free chocolate syrup over some fruit, sprinkle some semisweet chocolate chips into a bowl of cereal, or stir chocolate powder into yogurt. Or even try certain snacks sold in bulk, such as dark chocolate–covered almonds or raisins.

For some of us, giving up chocolate would be impossible. Rather than deny yourself the little indulgences that make you happy, try to incorporate them into your diet in a sparing and sensible way.

Chocolate-covered Raisins

- A handful of dark chocolate–covered raisins (say 15 or so) is equivalent to about 100 calories.

- You can also find chocolate-covered dried blueberries in certain gourmet shops, for a more special version of this snack.

Semisweet Chocolate Chips

- Semisweet chocolate chips can add a touch of sweetness to a bowl of frozen yogurt or even a bowl of cereal.

- Use the mini version and—surprise! you'll actually end up using less.

DRESSINGS, SAUCES, & DIPS

Changing the way you dress and dip can significantly reduce a meal's calories

Sometimes a salad is not as healthful as it seems. Depending on how much you dress it, you can add an extra 400 calories to a bowl of greens. But you don't need to drown your salad with vinaigrette. Not only is an overdressed salad overloaded with calories, but excess dressing also causes the greens to wilt prematurely. For a small salad, you only need about 2

tablespoons of dressing to coat it thoroughly.

Olive oil–based vinaigrettes, though high in calories, are packed with all the disease-fighting nutrients of olive oil. To get the flavor and benefits of these vinaigrettes without overdoing it on calories, transfer them to a pump and lightly spray your salad. Another technique involves serving your

Too Much Dressing

- This is the wrong way.

- Too often, we add more dressing to a salad than is needed.

- A quarter cup—even for a big salad—will drown the greens, adding excess calories *and* wilting the leaves.

Spraying Vinaigrette Instead

- This is the right way.

- Pumps like this one are available in kitchen stores and are great for vinaigrette.

- Make your own vinaigrette by combining olive oil, vinegar, and other ingredients, like lemon juice, roasted garlic, or hot mustard.

- Then pour the homemade vinaigrette into the pump, adding just a few sprays to your salad.

dressing in a small dipping dish on the side of your salad, and dipping each forkful of salad before eating it. This method will result in using less dressing than you would if you tossed the salad with it.

The same goes for sauces. Drowning your chicken in gravy or sauce is a good way to double the caloric value of a dish. Canned gravies can contain more than 100 calories per serving. Even condiments add 20–40 calories per tablespoon. So instead of drizzling with abandon, place the sauce in a small

dipping dish on the side and dip each forkful. You'll still get the flavor without excess.

You can lower the caloric value—while increasing the nutritional value—of sour cream–based dips by replacing the sour cream with plain nonfat Greek yogurt. This type of yogurt is thick and creamy; it's hard to believe it's fat free!

Cooking with fresh herbs and a variety of spices will result in your food having plenty of flavor, which means you won't need to add as much extra stuff to it.

Too Much Sauce

- This is the wrong way.

- Dumping this much sauce onto your dish could easily double the calories.

- Cooks who use too much sauce or gravy are usually trying to mask undesirable flavors in a poorly prepared dish.

Dipping Food Instead

- This is the right way.

- Prepare your food with the right amount of seasoning, using fresh herbs and various spices.

- If you still want to add a sauce, serve it on the side and dip each bite as you go.

DRINKS COUNT, TOO

Don't forget to include drinks in your day's calorie count. They add up!

Calories in, calories out refers to the number of calories you consume versus the number you expend. You may be good at keeping track of what you eat, but many of us don't think about the calories we drink. In fact, fruit juices, sodas, milk, coffee, and alcoholic beverages can account for up to half of our daily caloric intake and should be closely monitored.

If you like to enjoy fruit juice with breakfast, make sure you're drinking real juice, either fresh or from concentrate. Many fruit drinks contain added sugar and only a certain percentage of real fruit juice. You can also dilute your fruit juice with a bit of water or seltzer to make it all the more refreshing (and cut the number of calories in your glass).

Glass of Juice

- A cup of fresh orange or apple juice (an 8-ounce glass) contains 248 calories.

- Change your portion to a 6-ounce glass for just 186 calories. You can always top up with 2 ounces of water or seltzer.

Wine and Beer

- Do you like white or red? It matters.

- A 4-ounce glass of dry white wine contains about 77 calories.

- The same size glass of red or rosé is closer to 83 calories.

- A 12-ounce glass of beer can range from 110 calories for a light draft to 210 for a dark porter.

When it comes to sodas, you should be aware that these are just empty calories. While addictive to many, these drinks contain no nutritional value whatsoever. If you must indulge in an occasional can of soda, opt for the diet kind.

Most of us prefer to get our caffeine fix through a hot cup of coffee. The nutritional value of coffee has been debated over the years. While it contains just trace minerals that provide little nutrition, some studies have suggested that, in moderation, it may lower the risk of certain diseases, including colon cancer. The problem is that most of us like our coffee flavored with milk and sugar. Adding whole milk to your coffee can add more than 100 calories to an otherwise nearly calorie-free drink. If you prefer cream in your coffee, the caloric value can be even greater.

At the end of a long day, you may like to relax with a beer or want to sip a glass of wine with dinner. Be aware that, depending on your tipple of choice, you could be consuming hundreds of extra calories with each glass. While a glass of wine per day has been shown to have cardiovascular benefits, moderation is the key.

Can of Soda

- An 8-ounce glass of cola contains 96 calories and no nutrients.

- Be aware that a can of cola actually contains 12 ounces, which makes for 144 calories per can.

- Diet cola has no calories, but instead contains aspartame, an artificial sweetener.

Cup of Coffee

- The calories in a cup of coffee are negligible. But not all of us enjoy our coffee black.

- Adding milk, sugar, or cream to coffee ups its caloric value significantly.

- Top it with whipped cream, and you might as well call it dessert!

23

BAKING SUBSTITUTIONS

Swapping out some or all of the butter or lard in a recipe can cut significant calories

Replace butter with other fats to make delicious baked goods minus the calories. Butter has traditionally been the cornerstone of many a baking recipe. Oils and fat give cakes and pastries their texture and moistness. But you can replace ingredients like butter or reduce the amount of such ingredients in a given recipe to achieve the desired texture and flavor with far fewer calories. One easy way to cut the fat and calories in a cake is to replace the butter with yogurt. In some cases, you can replace all the butter with yogurt—usually by using half to three-quarters of the amount called for. You can also use half the amount of butter and replace the other half with yogurt.

Portion of Butter

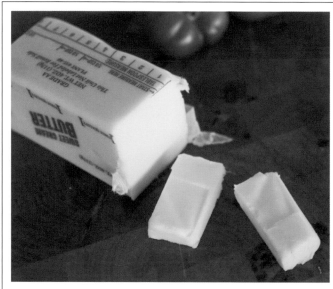

- A pat of butter is equivalent to about 5 grams and contains 36 calories.
- Baking recipes regularly call for ½ cup of butter or more, which accounts for at least 800 calories.

Replacing Butter with Yogurt

- Replacing butter with plain nonfat yogurt cuts the calorie and fat content tremendously.
- The tangy taste and extra protein are just two added benefits.

Recipes that call for shortening can also be modified to incorporate yogurt. Use three-quarters of the shortening called for and replace the last quarter with yogurt. Yogurt can also replace milk or water in a recipe for a creamier texture and increased protein content. It also adds a delightfully tangy taste to your final product.

Depending on the type of yogurt you use, you may need more or less than we've described to reach the desired consistency and flavor. Using plain nonfat Greek yogurt will allow you to use a little less than, say, a thinner American-style yogurt. Greek-style yogurt is thick and creamy. It contains 120 calories per cup compared to 1,628 calories for a cup of unsalted butter.

It has long been believed that replacing butter with margarine is a more healthful way of cooking. Regular margarine, which is a processed oil spread, can contain the same number of calories as butter. Fat-free versions can contain far less, but are still full of saturated fats and—worse—trans fats.

Mixing Yogurt into Batter

- Mix in your yogurt at the point when you would add butter or oil.

- Because yogurt is soft, you will have an easier time incorporating it.

- For recipes that call for cold cubed butter, use half the amount of butter called for and replace the second half with yogurt.

Lemon Loaf with Yogurt

- Lemon cake and muffin recipes lend themselves well to baking with yogurt.

- The tartness of the lemon is complemented by the tanginess of the yogurt.

25

USING EGG WHITES

When a recipe calls for eggs, you don't always need the yolks

Whether you're making an omelet or baking a cake, you're going to need eggs. But you may not need the entire egg. Sometimes just the whites will do. In other cases, one yolk combined with several whites will result in the right flavor and consistency.

When it comes to breakfast, eggs are a favorite. Egg-white omelets, however, can often be flimsy and flavorless. If egg-white omelets don't really tickle your fancy, why not try the one-egg omelet? It makes use of one whole egg plus two or three additional egg whites. The one yolk gives the omelet color and an eggy flavor, but without the calories of a three-egg omelet.

The same concept can be applied to baking. Eggs are used as emulsifiers in baking, and they help bind all the other ingredients together. When two eggs are required, you can replace one of them with two whites. When one egg is required, you

The Yolk Has ¾ of the Calories

- By removing the yolk from eggs, you're removing three-quarters of the calories contained in a whole egg.

- Removing the yolk can mean removing the taste or emulsifying effect of the egg.

- Play with replacing all but one of the yolks in a given recipe.

Separating Eggs

- Carefully crack the egg on the side of a bowl.

- Working over the bowl, carefully transfer the yolk back and forth between the two halves of the eggshell.

- As you do this, let the white of the egg leak down into the bowl.

- Be careful to keep the egg yolk intact as you do this.

can often use one or two egg whites in its place.

What's in an egg? Depending on how you cook them, eggs have varying caloric and nutritional values. A large raw egg has 54 calories, but if you scramble it, it has 102 because of the added milk. If you poach it, it has 71, and if you fry it, it has 90.

Packaged Egg Whites

- Buying packaged egg whites can be cheaper than buying whole eggs, especially if you're throwing away the yolks.

- You usually want to use ¼ cup of egg whites for each egg a recipe calls for.

Separating Eggs Another Way

- Another way to separate egg whites from yolks is to crack the egg using one hand.

- Gently separate the two halves of the eggshell, using your index finger and thumb to hold one half and your ring finger to secure the other half against your palm.

- Over a bowl, gently let the egg yolk and white slip into your other palm. The white will leak through your fingers, while the yolk sits in your palm.

SWEETENER SUBSTITUTIONS
Sugar is not always the sweetest way to sweeten a dish

For those of us trying to lose weight or maintain our weight, sugar is a controversial topic. On the one hand, pure granulated sugar is integral to many of the foods we enjoy and is not harmful in moderation. A teaspoon of sugar contains just 15 calories. The problem is that we tend to consume far too much sugar. Young people consume up to 8 tablespoons of sugar per day, which accounts for some 360 extra calories. Finding other ways to sweeten our favorite foods cannot

only cut calories in our diets, but fight the negative effects of overconsumption, which include the potential rise of cholesterol levels and the decline of immune health. Poor dental health is another risk of eating too much sugar.

One way to combat the effects of too much sugar is to replace it with an artificial sweetener. Several are available, including aspartame- and sucralose-based products. Splenda, for example, has made quite a name for itself as a

Splenda

- Splenda is an artificial sweetener made from sucralose.

- Splenda contains no calories, and has been shown to behave much like sugar when used in baking.

Applesauce

- Not only can fruit purees such as applesauce be used to replace sugar in cake and other pastry recipes, but the applesauce can also be used to replace some of the fat (butter or oil) in the recipe.

- Fruit purees can also be used as pie fillings or as bases for fruit sauces.

baking ingredient, as it can stand in for sugar with mostly the same results.

Other natural ingredients can also be used to replace sugar in baking. Baking with applesauce not only sweetens a dish but also allows you to use less fat, as the pectin in the applesauce moistens the final product.

Honey, although considered a healthier sweetener, is actually higher in calories than sugar because it's 100 percent sucrose. However, it boasts potential health benefits absent in plain white sugar. Honey contains enzymes and B vitamins that have been shown to boost the immune system. Also, because honey's sweeter than sugar, you don't have to use as much.

Honey

- Honey is a far sweeter sweetener than sugar.

- It's 100 percent sucrose, so it has more calories than regular sugar, but because it's so sweet, you don't need as much of it.

- Honey also boasts several nutritional properties, including natural antimicrobial characteristics.

Fruit Juice

- Fruit juice can replace sugar in certain baking recipes.

- In many cases, you can use frozen concentrated fruit juice in cakes, pastries, and cream toppings instead of plain sugar.

- Fruit juices not only sweeten a dish, but also add fruity notes to the flavor of the final product.

COCONUT-INFUSED FRENCH TOAST

Laced with coconut, this dish can be topped with fruit or enjoyed on its own

When making French toast, it's all about the bread. The final dish depends on whether you use a crusty French bread or a fluffy piece of challah. Even simple sandwich bread will do, so don't throw out those last few stale slices. Dip them in an eggy cinnamon- and coconut-infused mixture to make delicious French toast.

To handle your French toast, some people prefer to use a fork, while others like to use tongs. To best avoid over soaking your bread in the egg mixture or having part of it break off, hold two corners of each slice with your fingers, then quickly submerge each side.

Yield: 2 servings

Ingredients

1 egg plus 3 egg whites

¼ cup nonfat milk

3 tablespoons coconut milk

¼ teaspoon cinnamon

¼ teaspoon nutmeg

4 pieces stale whole wheat bread

½ cup chopped fresh pineapple

Calories 285, **Fat** (g) 10, **Carbohydrates** (g) 36, **Protein** (g) 16, **Fiber** (g) 5, **Saturated Fat** (g) 6, **Cholesterol** (mg) 106, **Sodium** (mg) 432

Coconut-infused French Toast

- In a large mixing bowl, combine the egg, milk, coconut milk, cinnamon, and nutmeg.

- Using a whisk, mix the ingredients together until well combined. Spray a large nonstick frying pan or skillet with olive oil. Take each slice of bread and dip it into the egg mixture. Be careful not to over soak it.

- Place the pan over medium-high heat. Let it heat up for a few minutes. Cook toast until golden brown on one side. Flip.

- Top the toast with pineapple and serve.

Fruit-topped French Toast: Dip four slices of bread into the egg mixture and fry on each side. Slice up ½ a cup of your favorite fresh tropical fruit—papaya, kiwi, or banana—and spoon onto your French toast before drizzling on a bit of maple syrup or honey.

Vanilla-infused French toast: Instead of using coconut, add vanilla to your egg mixture. Whisk together an egg and three egg whites with ¼ cup of milk, then add ½ teaspoon vanilla extract, ¼ teaspoon cinnamon, and ¼ teaspoon nutmeg. Dip four slices of bread into the egg mixture and fry on each side. Top with assorted fresh berries and a sprinkle of powdered sugar.

Dip Your Bread

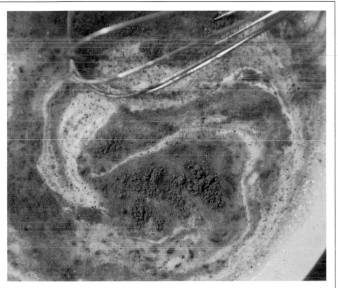

French Toast Frying

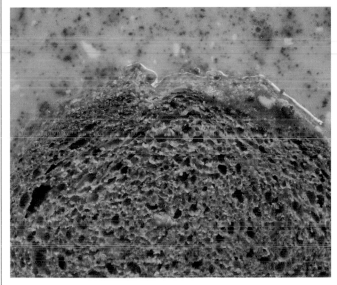

- When dipping the bread in the egg mixture, it's important not to overdo it.

- Cover each slice completely with egg mixture, but don't oversoak to the point of sogginess.

- Use your fingers to hold the corner of each slice as you dip.

- Alternatively, you can use tongs to hold the bread as you dip. Remember not to oversoak, or the slice will fall apart in the mixing bowl.

- Place each slice of dipped bread in the heated pan.

- Let the bread cook on each side for 2–3 minutes, or until browned on the outside and cooked through on the inside.

- You can test for doneness by gently piercing the center of the bread with a fork. If the fork comes out clean and dry, the toast is done.

- Remove each slice from the heat and transfer to a plate. Top with pineapple chunks and serve.

LEISURELY BREAKFAST

TEX-MEX SCRAMBLE

Veggies, beans, and cheese pack this scramble full of flavor

There's nothing easier than throwing a few fresh ingredients into a pan and frying them for breakfast. From truck stops to your mother's kitchen, scrambles are a breakfast favorite. Toss in whatever leftovers are lying around in the fridge or get creative with some fresh vegetables you picked up at the greenmarket or your favorite artisanal cheese.

This scramble is packed full of flavor and color and is sure to fill you up. Stuffed full of carbs, protein, and fresh nutrient-

rich veggies, our Tex-Mex Scramble makes for a balanced breakfast and is perfect for a lazy weekend morning.
Yield: 2 servings

Ingredients

1 egg plus 3 egg whites

Olive oil

¼ cup diced onion

¼ cup diced green bell pepper

¼ cup canned black beans, rinsed

¼ cup diced plum tomato

3 ounces grated Pepper Jack cheese

Sea salt and freshly ground pepper, to taste

Calories 252, **Fat** (g) 15, **Carbohydrates** (g) 9, **Protein** (g) 21, **Fiber** (g) 3, **Saturated Fat** (g) 9, **Cholesterol** (mg) 150, **Sodium** (mg) 604

Tex-Mex Scramble

- In a large mixing bowl, whisk egg and egg whites until smooth. Spray a nonstick frying pan or skillet with oil; heat it over medium-high heat before beginning to cook.

- Add onion to pan and cook. Stir in the pepper and cook for a few minutes.

- Add beans and tomatoes, stirring everything together well.

- Pour eggs into the pan. Stir in so that the eggs cook evenly with the other ingredients.

- Add cheese, season to taste, and serve.

Tex-Mex Tofu Scramble: Try using tofu instead of eggs. If you are new to tofu, a tofu scramble can be a great introduction to the ingredient. Use extra-firm tofu for best results. Sauté your veggies as you would for a regular scramble, then crumble the tofu over the top. Be careful not to mash it up as you "scramble" it together. Cook for 10–15 minutes, or until the tofu has softened and looks like scrambled eggs.

Tip: Save the leftover scramble to wrap in a tortilla for a quick breakfast burrito on the go. Spoon the scramble into a tortilla, tuck in the ends and fold the tortilla over, and then pop the whole thing in the microwave for 30 seconds.

Veggies and Beans Cooking

Sprinkle in the Cheese

- Cook the onion and bell pepper until they soften.

- The cooked onions should be translucent in color.

- The beans should be rinsed with cold water in a colander before using.

- While the eggs are still cooking, sprinkle in the cheese, salt, and pepper.

- Allow the eggs to cook through, stirring the scramble as you go.

- Remove the scramble from the heat and, using a spatula, transfer to a plate. Serve.

LEISURELY BREAKFAST

SPINACH & RICOTTA OMELET

Wake up to this colorful omelet stuffed with nutrient-rich spinach and milky ricotta cheese

We traditionally eat omelets for breakfast, but they can be enjoyed at any meal. Serve your omelet with a salad for a light lunch or alongside roasted vegetables for an easy dinner.

This omelet, filled with spinach and ricotta cheese, is light and nutritious. Using one egg yolk gives it more color and flavor than an all egg-white omelet. Beating the egg and egg whites vigorously will ensure a fluffy end result. The spinach infuses the dish with nutrients, and the ricotta gives it a tangy cheesiness. Of course, the beauty of the omelet is that you can add whatever you like to it. We've included a few variations here.

Yield: 1

Ingredients

1 teaspoon olive oil

¼ cup diced red onion

½ cup roughly chopped baby spinach

⅓ cup low-fat ricotta

1 egg plus 3 egg whites

Sea salt and freshly ground pepper, to taste

Spinach and Ricotta Omelet

- Heat oil in a nonstick frying pan or skillet over medium-high heat.

- Sauté onion until soft and translucent. Stir in the spinach and sauté until it's wilted.

- Remove pan from heat; combine the spinach and onion mixture with the ricotta in a mixing bowl.

- Beat and cook eggs. Add the ricotta mixture. Season, fold, and serve.

Calories 285, **Fat** (g) 16, **Carbohydrates** (g) 10, **Protein** (g) 24, **Fiber** (g) 1, **Saturated Fat** (g) 6, **Cholesterol** (mg) 237, **Sodium** (mg) 617

Spinach & Feta Cheese Omelet: To slightly alter the flavors in the omelet, use ⅓ cup feta cheese instead of ricotta. Crumble it into the sautéed spinach and onion, then spoon it into your cooking omelet. Feta is saltier, so you probably won't need to add salt to the egg mixture.

Kale & Ricotta Omelet: You can also swap out spinach for kale, which adds an extra fiber kick to the dish. You'll have to sauté the kale a minute or two longer than the spinach, as it's a more robust green.

Cook Eggs

Fold the Omelet

- In a mixing bowl, beat the egg and egg whites until smooth and foamy. The foamier the egg mixture, the fluffier your omelet will be.

- Lightly spray a frying pan with olive oil and, over medium-high heat, pour in the egg. Rotate the pan while folding in the edges of the omelet so that it cooks evenly throughout.

- When the egg is 70–80 percent firm, scoop the spinach and ricotta mixture on top and sprinkle with salt and pepper to taste.

- Folding the omelet can be tricky. To prevent it from sticking, run the tines of a fork along the edge of the omelet.

- Slide a spatula carefully under one half of the omelet and fold it in half.

- Allow the omelet to cook for another minute or so, then turn it.

- Allow the omelet to cook for another minute, then tip the pan to gently slide it onto a plate.

LEISURELY BREAKFAST

TOAD IN A HOLE

Regardless of what you call it, this kids' breakfast is fun for all ages

This children's favorite goes by many names: Egg in a House, Egg in a Basket, Egg Toast, etc. We like to use the bread hole cutout as a little top hat to help sop up the runny yolk (and so that it doesn't go to waste). To make this kid-friendly dish a little more grown up, we've added fresh herbs, which add nutrients to the final result as well as a little extra zing to the dish.

You'll need a regular circular cookie cutter for this dish. If you don't have one, you can always use a plastic cup with a diameter of about two inches.
Yield: 1

Ingredients

Olive oil

2 slices whole wheat bread

2 eggs

¼ cup fresh parsley, finely chopped

Sea salt and freshly ground pepper, to taste

Calories 332, **Fat** (g) 12, **Carbohydrates** (g) 32, **Protein** (g) 20, **Fiber** (g) 2, **Saturated Fat** (g) 4, **Cholesterol** (mg) 424, **Sodium** (mg) 808

Toad in a Hole

- Spray a nonstick frying pan or skillet with olive oil and place over medium-high heat.

- Cut holes in bread. Place each slice of bread in the pan and cook 2 minutes.

- Flip bread; cook for another 2 minutes on the other side.

- Crack the eggs into the bread holes.

- Sprinkle the eggs with parsley, salt, and pepper, then cook for 2–3 minutes. Flip and cook 2 minutes. Serve with toasted "hats."

Toad in a Hole with Thyme: Instead of parsley, finely chop up ¼ cup fresh thyme to sprinkle on top of your Toad in a Hole. Thyme, which is an ideal seasoning for chicken, can also bring eggs to life. The herb has long been used medicinally and it boasts antimicrobial properties.

Spicy Toad in a Hole: People often like hot sauce with their eggs. Toss a dash or two of Tabasco or your favorite hot sauce in with the raw egg as you crack it into the hole to spice up your breakfast.

Cut Holes in Bread

- To make the holes, twist a circular cookie cutter into the center of each slice of bread.

- Remove the circles of bread and set aside.

- Spray both sides of each slice of bread lightly with olive oil. Cook the slices of bread separately, as it gets tricky once you add the "toad," or egg.

- Toss hole cutouts into the pan to toast for a few minutes on each side. Use as "hats" on top of the finished dish.

Work with the Egg

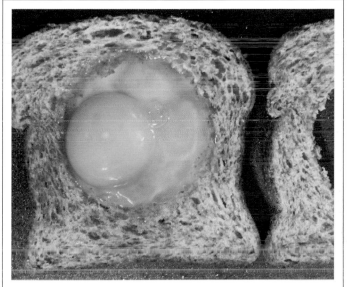

- Working with the egg can be tricky. Carefully crack the egg into the bread hole.

- Slip a spatula under the bread and flip the whole thing over.

- Once the second side is cooked, gently slide the spatula under the bread to ensure the egg has not stuck to the pan.

- Angle the pan to slide the toad in a hole onto a plate. Serve with the "hat" on top.

PARISIAN-STYLE CREPES

Bring the City of Light to your breakfast table with these simple crepes

What we think of as breakfast food is enjoyed as a snack purchased from street vendors in Paris. Whip up these crepes in the morning or any time of day for a Parisian-style snack. You can keep what you don't eat in a plastic container in the fridge and take one out to heat up in the microwave at your leisure.

The traditional Parisian style, of course, is simply to sprinkle with a little lemon and sugar. But topping your crepes with fresh fruit or infusing them with zesty flavors can brighten your breakfast and boost the nutritional value of your crepes.

Yield: 1

Ingredients

¹/₂ cup all-purpose flour

1 egg

¹/₂ cup nonfat milk

1 tablespoon sugar

¹/₂ teaspoon vanilla extract

¹/₄ teaspoon salt

Olive oil

Half a lemon

Granulated or confectioners' sugar

Parisian-style Crepes

- In a mixing bowl, combine flour, egg, milk, sugar, vanilla, and salt, whisking until smooth.

- Spray an 8-inch nonstick pan with olive oil and place over medium-high heat. Pour in disks of batter about 3 inches in diameter.

- Rotate pan at an angle to spread the batter as thin and evenly as possible.

- Cook each crepe until bubbles start to appear. Then flip it and cook for another minute before removing from heat. Sprinkle with lemon juice and sugar, and serve.

Calories 350, **Fat** (g) 6, **Carbohydrates** (g) 56, **Protein** (g) 17, **Fiber** (g) 2, **Saturated Fat** (g) 2, **Cholesterol** (mg) 214, **Sodium** (mg) 717

• • • • RECIPE VARIATIONS • • • •

Fruit Crepes: To boost the flavor and nutrition of these crepes, slice up ½ cup of strawberries and fold them into the crepes. You can also use raspberries, blueberries, sliced bananas, or a combination of any of these to stuff your crepes.

Ginger Crepes: Instead of vanilla, add ½ teaspoon of grated ginger and 2 tablespoons of orange juice to your egg mixture. You won't have to top your crepes with anything: They'll be infused with flavor—and a natural anti-inflammatory from the ginger.

Forming the Crepes

Finish the Crepe

- Don't worry about making your crepes as thin as possible. The important part is that they cook evenly.

- The key is in the rotation of the pan. Pour a small amount of batter into the pan and immediately rotate the pan, holding it at an angle.

- Spray your pan with oil between crepes so that they don't stick to the pan.

- When getting ready to flip your crepe, run your spatula along the edges to ensure that it isn't sticking, then slide the spatula underneath and flip.

- Don't worry about the early crepes cooling as you make the rest. Simply keep piling fresh, warm crepes on top of the others to keep them warm.

- To prevent the crepes from sticking to each other, roll them into loose cigars as you pile them up.

- To finish a crepe, squeeze a wedge of lemon over its surface and sprinkle it with a little sugar.

- Fold the crepe over twice, forming a quarter circle, or roll it into a cigar, and serve.

ITALIAN BAKED EGGS

Fresh tomatoes, basil, and mozzarella add pizzazz to baked eggs

Baked eggs are found in both France and Italy. Prepared in individual baking dishes, they're like mini crustless quiches with runny yolks. For the individual baking dishes, use ramekins (mostly used for crème brûlée and molten cakes) or custard cups. French onion soup bowls work, too.

This light and colorful version of the dish incorporates fresh tomatoes, peppery basil, and milky mozzarella, as well as balsamic vinegar for a touch of tang.

Layer your tomatoes, basil, mozzarella, and eggs so that the cheese melts evenly as it cooks. This way, you'll get a bit of it in each delicious forkful.

Yield: 1

KNACK CALORIE COUNTER COOKBOOK

Ingredients

Olive oil

3 ounces fresh buffalo mozzarella, sliced into thin disks

³/₄ cup cherry or grape tomatoes, halved

1 tablespoon balsamic vinegar

¹/₄ cup finely chopped fresh basil

2 eggs

Sea salt and freshly ground pepper, to taste

Toast (optional)

Calories 342, **Fat** (g) 20, **Carbohydrates** (g) 6, **Protein** (g) 30, **Fiber** (g) 2, **Saturated Fat** (g) 12, **Cholesterol** (mg) 272, **Sodium** (mg) 736

Italian Baked Eggs

- Spray an individual baking dish with olive oil.

- Place the mozzarella on the bottom of the dish, scatter the tomatoes on top, then sprinkle in the vinegar.

- Carefully crack the eggs into the dish, and top with basil, salt, and pepper.

- In an oven preheated to 400°F, cook for 20 minutes or until set. Remove and let sit for a couple of minutes before serving with a wedge of toast.

ZOOM

Change up the flavors in this dish by using different herbs and a different cheese. Instead of basil,
finely chop up cilantro to add to the dish. You can
also try switching mozzarella for fontina, which has
a stronger taste and melts more like cheddar.

• • • • • RECIPE VARIATION • • • • •

French Baked Eggs: Make this dish more French than
Italian by changing up the ingredients. Use 2 ounces
of grated Gruyère instead of an Italian cheese. And
replace the basil with 2 tablespoons of dried herbes
de Provence. Instead of cherry tomatoes, thinly slice
up half a large beefsteak tomato and half a small green
zucchini to layer with the cheese, herbs and eggs.

Layer Tomatoes and Mozzarella

Crack Eggs into Dish

- If using fresh buffalo mozzarella, slice it into ¼-inch-
  thick disks and lay these
  out on the bottom of the
  individual baking dish.

- You can also use bocconcini, which are mini buffalo
  mozzarella balls, roughly
  the same size as grape
  tomatoes.

- If using bocconcini, simply
  halve them as you do the
  tomatoes and layer the two.

- As you carefully crack the
  eggs into the individual
  baking dish, the whites will
  leak down into the layers of
  tomatoes and cheese.

- To ensure your eggs cook
  evenly, place your bak-
  ing dish in a shallow pan
  of water. This will create
  steam, effectively poaching

the eggs as they bake.

- Don't wait until the eggs
  look firm. Bake them
  until the egg whites cook
  through and become an
  opaque white.

HOMEMADE INSTANT OATMEAL
Store this oatmeal in individual packets for easy access

A bowl of oatmeal in the morning is not only warm and comforting, but it's also a great source of dietary fiber and protein, as well as vitamin E, zinc, selenium, copper, iron, manganese, and magnesium.

You can buy instant oatmeal already packaged, but making your own individual servings of oatmeal ensures that you know exactly what you're eating. Homemade oatmeal means no processed additives and no preservatives.

Prepare your instant oatmeal mixture, and then store it in sandwich baggies or small sealable plastic containers. Then you can just add hot water to one serving or take it to go as a healthy snack.

Yield: 8 servings

Ingredients

4 cups quick-cooking oats

3 tablespoons brown sugar

2 teaspoons cinnamon

1 teaspoon salt

1/2 cup dried apples

Calories 184, **Fat** (g) 3, **Carbohydrates** (g) 35, **Protein** (g) 7, **Fiber** (g) 5, **Saturated Fat** (g) 0.5, **Cholesterol** (mg) 0.0, **Sodium** (mg) 299

Homemade Instant Oatmeal

- In a large mixing bowl, combine all the ingredients and mix well.

- Divide the mixture into eight parts and store in sandwich baggies or sealable plastic containers.

- When you're ready for a quick breakfast, pour roughly 1 cup of hot water (depending on your desired consistency) over a serving of the oatmeal mixture in a bowl.

- Allow the oatmeal to set for several minutes and serve as is or with fresh fruit slices.

Fruit & Nut Instant Oatmeal: Instead of dried apples, use ½ cup dried cranberries, blueberries, or raisins. You can also add just ¼ cup of dried fruit and a ¼ of chopped nuts, such as almonds or walnuts, to the quick-cooking oats.

Maple Pecan Oatmeal: Infuse your oatmeal with a touch of maple sweetness. Instead of brown sugar, stir 3 tablespoons of grade B or higher pure maple syrup into the quick-cooking oats. Add ½ cup of chopped pecans to the mixture.

Using Brown Sugar

One Serving

- Brown sugar has a tendency to become hard in storage. To remedy this, simply use a terra cotta disk or terra cotta bear, sold in kitchen stores.

- Soak the terra cotta in water for a few minutes.

- Place the disk on top of your sugar. Within 20 minutes, the sugar will soften.

- You can also use a piece of stale bread or dried apple slices to achieve the same result. Place them on top of your sugar to soften it.

- Small sandwich bags are ideal for storing your oatmeal servings.

- You can also use small sealable plastic containers.

- Sealable tin containers are lightweight and perfect for storing your oatmeal servings.

43

QUICK BREAKFAST

EGGS & SOLDIERS

A touch of spice and sweetness turns plain toast into a treat

Another kids' favorite, Eggs & Soldiers is also a fun and tasty breakfast for grown-ups. It consists of soft-boiled eggs and toasted bread strips for dipping.

As with other recipes that call for toast, the type of bread you use makes all the difference. Try a hearty rye bread like pumpernickel for your soldiers, or even a sourdough.

In any case, you should try to use a whole wheat bread. When you eat white bread, almost half of the nutrients contained in the original grain have been removed. What is removed includes the bran and germ of the wheat grain, which are its most nutritious parts, as well as more than half of the vitamin B_1, B_2, and B_3; vitamin E; folic acid; calcium; phosphorus; zinc; copper; iron; and fiber.

Yield: 1

Ingredients

2 eggs

Sea salt and freshly ground pepper, to taste

1 piece whole wheat toast, cut into strips

Calories 278, **Fat** (g) 12, **Carbohydrates** (g) 26, **Protein** (g) 18, **Fiber** (g) 4, **Saturated Fat** (g) 4, **Cholesterol** (mg) 424, **Sodium** (mg) 704

Eggs & Soldiers

- In a pot, bring a quart of water to a boil. Using a spoon, slide the eggs into the boiling water and cook for 3 minutes.

- Remove the eggs and place each in an eggcup. Using a spoon, gently crack off the top of each egg, then use a paring knife to lightly scrape the white from the shell.

- Sprinkle salt and pepper onto the eggs and serve with toast strips.

MAKE IT EASY

To get the best results with this dish, go for an extra large egg. Smaller eggs will be difficult to dip your soldiers into. A larger egg will be easier to crack the top off of, and will give just that much more room for dipping.

Cracking the Egg

- To crack the top of an egg off, begin by placing it in an eggcup. If you don't have one, you can use a shot glass or similarly sized receptacle.

- Using a spoon or knife, gently strike the egg about two-thirds of the way up.

- Remove the top, then use a spoon or paring knife to scoop out the white in the top part.

Separating Egg from Shell

- Carefully edge a paring knife along the inside walls of the egg to loosen the white.

- With the white of the egg loosened, you'll have an easier time scooping all the insides out.

- To eat, dip the bread strips into the soft-boiled egg.

CINNAMON TOAST

Easy peasy cinnamon toast is a breakfast favorite for kids and grownups of all ages

It might sound like the easiest (and quickest) breakfast idea, but don't write off Cinnamon Toast. The savory-sweet dish can be whipped up in seconds, but boasts several important nutrients.

Not only is whole wheat bread an excellent source of fiber, but studies have shown that eating ½ teaspoon of cinnamon every day can lower cholesterol. Cinnamon also has an anti-clotting effect on the blood and, when added to foods, has been shown to prevent bacterial growth and food spoilage, making it a natural preservative.

Enjoy it on its own or with a side of yogurt that you can use as a tangy dip. *Yield: 1*

KNACK CALORIE COUNTER COOKBOOK

Ingredients

2 slices whole wheat bread

2 small pats butter

2 teaspoons sugar

1 teaspoon cinnamon

Cinnamon Toast

- Lightly toast the bread in a toaster.

- Butter it while it's still hot.

- Sprinkle on sugar and cinnamon.

Calories 243, **Fat** (g) 10, **Carbohydrates** (g) 36, **Protein** (g) 4, **Fiber** (g) 2, **Saturated Fat** (g) 6, **Cholesterol** (mg) 22, **Sodium** (mg) 399

Cinnamon Toast & Dip: Spruce up your Cinnamon Toast by dipping it into a flavored yogurt. In a bowl, combine ¾ cup of plain nonfat Greek yogurt with ½ teaspoon of vanilla and ½ teaspoon of sugar. Whip the ingredients together until they're well incorporated, and serve alongside your toast.

Cinnamon Toast & Fruit Yogurt: Serve your Cinnamon Toast with a fruity yogurt for dipping. Combine ¾ cup yogurt with 1 tablespoon of your favorite fruit jam. Mix the two together until well combined, then dip at your own leisure.

Grinding Your Own Cinnamon

Measuring Using Your Pinky

- Ground cinnamon can go stale in a few months, but cinnamon sticks retain their flavor for a year or more.

- To grind your own, break up a stick and toss a piece of it into a coffee grinder.

- Buy a separate grinder to use especially for spices—

don't use the same grinder you use for coffee beans.

- Alternatively, you can grind cinnamon the old-fashioned way using a mortar and pestle. Break up a stick into the mortar. Work the pestle firmly until the cinnamon is a fine powder.

- To determine how much cinnamon to use without an actual measuring tool, you can simply eyeball it.

- A teaspoon of cinnamon is about equivalent to the size of the tip of your pinky finger.

47

GRANOLA & YOGURT PARFAIT
Layer this easy granola with yogurt for a perfect parfait

Granola is one of those healthy meals that can be eaten at any time, anywhere. Making your own granola at home is easy and efficient, as it cuts down on unnecessary packaging and waste. Make enough for the week, then store it in a sealable plastic container to use as needed. You can add milk to the granola to enjoy it as cereal, but we love this granola and yogurt parfait, which can be eaten at home or on the go as a portable breakfast or a healthy snack.

You can add any number of dried fruits or nuts to your granola, but keep in mind that the concentrated sugars in dried fruit and the good fats in nuts make it a filling meal. In other words, a little goes a long way and half a cup of granola is plenty.

Yield: 6 servings

Ingredients

3 cups rolled oats

$\frac{1}{2}$ cup coconut flakes

$\frac{1}{2}$ cup raw chopped or slivered almonds

$\frac{1}{4}$ cup vegetable oil

$\frac{1}{4}$ cup honey

1 teaspoon sea salt

1 teaspoon vanilla extract

1 cup dried cranberries

3 cups plain nonfat Greek yogurt

Calories 465, **Fat** (g) 22, **Carbohydrates** (g) 56, **Protein** (g) 15, **Fiber** (g) 6, **Saturated Fat** (g) 0, **Cholesterol** (mg) 106, **Sodium** (mg) 406

Homemade Granola & Yogurt Parfait

- Combine all the ingredients, except for the dried cranberries and yogurt, and mix well.

- On a nonstick cookie sheet, spread out the mixture evenly.

- In an oven preheated to 350°F, bake the granola for 25–30 minutes. Turn the oats over every 10 minutes.

- Remove from the oven and let cool. Transfer to a mixing bowl and add the dried cranberries.

- Layer one-sixth of the granola with ½ cup of plain or fruit-flavored nonfat yogurt.

Fruit & Nut Granola: Use any raw nuts or dried fruits in your granola. Try 1 cup of pistachios, cashews, or walnuts, or a combination of any of these, along with 1 cup of dried cherries, dried blueberries, or raisins.

Mixing the Raw Ingredients

Adding the Cranberries

- Stir the mixture until the oats are well coated with the oil and honey and the other ingredients are well dispersed.

- Add the dried cranberries after the granola has baked, otherwise they will become gummy and stick to the other ingredients.

- It's important to let the granola cool before adding the cranberries so that the cranberries don't become gummy and stick together.

- After the granola is baked and cooled, put it in a mixing bowl and add the dried cranberries.

- Toss the mixture, using your hands to make sure that the cranberries are well dispersed throughout the mixture.

QUICK BREAKFAST

GREEK YOGURT, FRUIT, & HONEY

This Mediterranean-style breakfast is light and easy

When it comes to yogurt, plain nonfat and Greek-style plain nonfat are like night and day. While plain yogurt can be thin and liquidy, Greek yogurt is thick and creamy. It's great to use in dips to replace sour cream for a healthier snack, as well as to eat on its own. This easy dish calls for plain nonfat Greek yogurt and honey, as well as a few slices of fresh peaches, something like a healthy version of peaches and cream.

Not only does Greek-style yogurt taste completely different,

it also boasts slightly more protein than regular nonfat yogurt. Plain nonfat Greek-style yogurt has 2.5 grams of protein per ounce compared to 1.5 grams of protein per ounce of plain nonfat American-style yogurt. And, while the American has a couple calories less than Greek-style, it also has twice as much sugar.

Yield: 1

Ingredients

1 cup plain nonfat Greek yogurt

2 tablespoons honey

$^{1}/_{2}$ cup sliced peaches

$^{1}/_{4}$ cup chopped raw almonds

Greek Yogurt, Fruit, & Honey

- Scoop the yogurt into a bowl.

- Drizzle on honey.

- Sprinkle sliced fruit and chopped nuts over the top.

Calories 493, **Fat** (g) 18, **Carbohydrates** (g) 72, **Protein** (g) 20, **Fiber** (g) 5, **Saturated Fat** (g) 4, **Cholesterol** (mg) 15, **Sodium** (mg) 178

Instead of almonds, add ¼ cup of a different type of nut to the dish. Walnuts or cashews can be roughly chopped and sprinkled on top. Cashews, in particular, are lower in fat than other types of nuts. And the fats they do contain are mostly unsaturated fatty acids, including oleic acid, which has been found to lower the risk of heart disease. Instead of using peaches, try this dish with ½ cup of sliced fresh ripe figs, which are native to Greece and pair wonderfully with Greek yogurt. These plump, fleshy fruits are an excellent source of potassium, and pretty when sliced in half to reveal their pink insides.

Slicing Peaches

- When choosing peaches for this dish, select ripe ones. You'll know they're ripe if pressing down on the skin leaves an imprint. We recommend leaving the skins on, as this is where many of the nutrients lie.

- Using a paring knife, slice the peach in half, stopping at the pit. Rotate the peach until you have sliced all the way around.

- Remove the pit using your fingers. You may have to loosen it with the knife.

- Slice each half into ¼-inch-thick wedges.

Chopping Almonds

- When a recipe calls for chopped almonds, you can usually buy the almonds already chopped.

- If you want to chop your own, use a sharp, heavy chef's knife for the job.

- On a cutting board, gather the nuts in a small circle. Firmly rock the knife back and forth over them, gathering those that have scattered, until the pieces are all roughly the same size.

EGGS & BACON SALAD

Eggs and bacon: together at last . . . in a salad!

You love bacon and eggs with toast. So why not toss them into a salad? This version of a classic breakfast is light in both calories and spirit. Incorporating baby spinach and cherry tomatoes, it's rich in antioxidants, as many colorful foods are. The spinach is high in calcium, iron, and vitamin K, which is important to the health of our bones.

Tomatoes are a great source of beta-carotene and other carotenoids, which can help prevent heart disease and cancer. A juicy red tomato is also high in vitamin C and potassium.

The bacon—in this case, a turkey bacon—and eggs, of course, provide the protein in this satisfying morning meal. *Yield: 1*

Ingredients

2 strips turkey bacon

1 egg

3 cups fresh baby spinach

1 cup cherry tomatoes, halved

½ cucumber, sliced

2 tablespoons olive oil

1 tablespoon balsamic vinegar

Freshly ground pepper, to taste

Calories 431, **Fat** (g) 36, **Carbohydrates** (g) 9, **Protein** (g) 22, **Fiber** (g) 4, **Saturated Fat** (g) 5, **Cholesterol** (mg) 261, **Sodium** (mg) 625

Eggs & Bacon Salad

- Spray a skillet with oil and cook turkey bacon over high heat until browned. Remove from heat, let cool, and chop.

- Poach egg. In a bowl, toss the spinach, tomatoes, cucumber, and bacon pieces with oil and vinegar.

- You can also use a pump of vinaigrette. (The poached egg's runny yolk will mix with the salad, so you needn't drown the salad in dressing as well.)

- Make a crater in the salad, and place the egg on top. Serve with a sprinkle of freshly ground pepper.

Bacon & Egg Chard Salad: Change up this salad by replacing the baby spinach with 3 cups young Swiss chard leaves. Chard has many of the same health benefits as spinach, plus a healthy dose of fiber. The bitter taste of Swiss chard will be tempered by the saltiness of the bacon and the creaminess of the egg yolk.

Canadian Bacon & Egg Salad: For a lean alternative to turkey bacon, you need not shy away from actual pork. Canadian bacon is made from the loin of the animal and, therefore, leaner than regular bacon. Use two strips of Canadian bacon in this salad for a smokier, heartier result.

Poaching an Egg

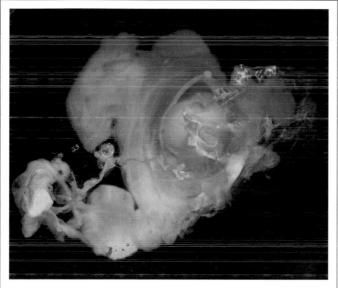

- To poach your egg, bring a medium-size pot of water to a boil over high heat. Then reduce the heat to low.

- Adding a teaspoon of vinegar to the pot will help the egg keep its shape.

- Crack an egg into a bowl, then carefully slide the egg from the bowl to the pot, being careful to avoid too much splashing.

- Cook the egg for 3–4 minutes. Then, using a large slotted spoon, scoop up the egg and serve immediately.

Preparing Bacon

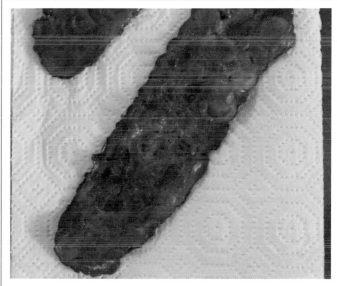

- Once the turkey bacon has cooked, remove it from heat and place the pieces on a paper towel to soak up the excess grease.

- Once the bacon has cooled, chop it into ¼-inch pieces and set aside.

QUICK BREAKFAST

53

LOW-FAT BLUEBERRY MUFFINS
Use yogurt instead of butter for muffins with a fraction of the fat

We like to think of muffins as healthful, but the fact is that they are actually a type of cake. (The word itself either comes from the French *moufflet*, which is a kind of soft bread, or from *muffet*, which is a kind of German cake.) Many muffins have a high fat content because of the ingredients used to make them.

But you can make your muffins more nutritious by replacing the butter most recipes call for with nonfat Greek yogurt, and by replacing half the all-purpose flour with whole wheat flour. Enjoy these delicious treats for a quick breakfast on the go.

Yield: 12

Ingredients

1 1/2 cups plain nonfat Greek yogurt

1/2 cup all-natural applesauce

2 eggs

2 teaspoons lemon juice

1 teaspoon vanilla extract

1 cup whole wheat flour

1 cup all-purpose flour

1 teaspoon grated fresh lemon zest

1 teaspoon baking powder

1/2 teaspoon baking soda

1/2 teaspoon salt

1 cup fresh or frozen blueberries

Calories 110, **Fat** (g) 1, **Carbohydrates** (g) 20, **Protein** (g) 6, **Fiber** (g) 3, **Saturated Fat** (g) 0, **Cholesterol** (mg) 36, **Sodium** (mg) 227

Low-fat Blueberry Muffins

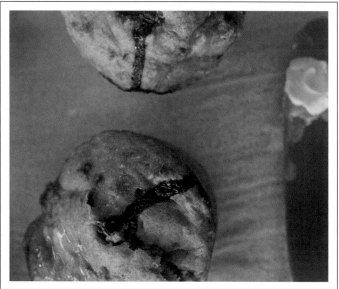

- In a mixing bowl, combine all wet ingredients and whisk together until well incorporated.

- A little at a time, add the dry ingredients to the wet, and mix together until you have a smooth batter.

- Add blueberries to the batter. Pour the batter into greased muffin tins.

- In an oven preheated to 350°F, bake muffins for 20–25 minutes or until tops are golden brown. Remove muffins from the tins. Let them cool on a rack for a few minutes before serving.

• • • • RECIPE VARIATIONS • • • •

Raspberry Muffins: Instead of using blueberries, add 1 cup fresh or frozen raspberries to your batter. You can also use 1 cup of a combination of blueberries, raspberries, and other fruits of the forest for a delicious mixed berry muffin.

Blueberry Orange Muffins: Instead of the lemon juice, add 1 tablespoon of fresh squeezed orange juice to the mixture. In addition, mix in one teaspoon of freshly grated orange zest in order to infuse the muffin batter with a zingy orange flavor.

Adding Blueberries to Batter

- Before you add the blueberries, check for any damaged berries and discard.

- Add the blueberries to the batter after combining the wet and dry ingredients.

- Make sure the berries are well dispersed throughout the batter, but mix gently to avoid damaging them.

Pouring Batter into Tins

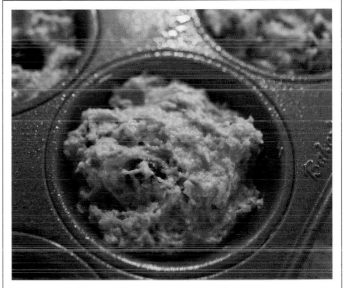

- Pour mixed batter into muffin tins sprayed with vegetable oil.

- Fill the muffin cups only about three-quarters full, to allow the muffins space to rise.

- Once the tins are removed from the oven and cooled, you can pop the muffins out of the cups.

CRAN-APRICOT SCONES

Enjoy these scones for breakfast or with afternoon tea

When you think of scones, you probably can't help but think of jam and clotted cream. Enjoy these low-cal scones with nonfat yogurt and fruit puree, or instead of dipping them in yogurt, spread on some low-fat cream cheese and your favorite fruit jam. Of course, they're best enjoyed just a little warm, so it's nice to pop them in the oven (at 250ºF for just a few minutes to lightly toast them) or the microwave (for just a few seconds on a medium setting) before eating them.

If you must enjoy tea with your scones, opt for a green tea that's packed with antioxidants, or even a young white tea, which studies have shown has immune-boosting properties.

Yield: 16

Ingredients

1 cup all-purpose flour

1 cup whole wheat flour

6 tablespoons sugar

¹/₂ teaspoon baking soda

1 teaspoon baking powder

¹/₄ teaspoon salt

4 tablespoons unsalted butter, chilled and cubed

¹/₄ cup dried apricots

¹/₄ cup dried cranberries

³/₄ cup plain low-fat yogurt

2 teaspoons grated fresh orange zest

1 egg plus 1 egg white

Calories 106, **Fat** (g) 4, **Carbohydrates** (g) 16, **Protein** (g) 3, **Fiber** (g) 2, **Saturated Fat** (g) 2, **Cholesterol** (mg) 22, **Sodium** (mg) 123

Cran-apricot Scones

- Combine all the dry ingredients. Blend in the cold butter until the mixture is crumbly in texture.

- Toss in the dried fruit, mixing everything together using your hands. In another mixing bowl, combine the yogurt, orange zest, and eggs and whisk together until smooth.

- Combine the mixtures, then knead the dough and form the scones.

- Sprinkle the dough pieces with sugar, and bake in a preheated 400°F oven for 15–18 minutes or until lightly browned.

•••• RECIPE VARIATIONS ••••

Fresh Fruit Scones: Replace the dried fruit with ¾ cup fresh berries, sliced stone fruits, apples, or chopped nuts. Simply combine the dry ingredients with the wet ingredients, then add the fresh fruit or nuts. Mix everything together well before spooning golf-ball-size pieces of the dough onto a cookie sheet and baking at 400°F for 15–18 minutes.

Lemon & Poppy Seed Scones: Rather than fill your scones with fruit chunks, infuse them with a zesty citrus flavor. Replace the orange zest with 2 tablespoons of lemon juice and 1 teaspoon of freshly grated lemon zest. Add these to the plain batter and blend well.

Kneading the Dough

- Once both the wet and dry mixtures are made, spoon the dry mixture, little by little, into the wet, mixing well until a dough with a slightly sticky consistency is formed.

- Place the dough on a lightly floured surface and gently knead it for several minutes.

Forming the Scones

- Form the dough into four separate balls, then break each ball into four pieces.

- Using a spoon (you may want to lightly oil or butter it to prevent the dough from sticking), spoon golf-ball-size pieces of dough onto a nonstick cookie sheet.

BANANA-BERRY SMOOTHIE

This satisfying smoothie allows you to take your breakfast in a to-go cup

By tossing a few ingredients into a blender, you can easily whip up a healthy, easy, and portable morning meal. This recipe calls for fresh fruit, juice, and milk. But you can boost the nutrient content of your smoothie by adding flaxseed, which is packed with omega-3s, spirulina for a protein punch, or wheatgrass to boost your metabolism. For a vegan smoothie, replace the nonfat milk with soy or rice milk. You can purchase flaxseed, spirulina, and wheatgrass at health food stores or even at the supermarket or pharmacy. If using flax, a teaspoon will do. For spirulina, add a tablespoon, and for wheatgrass, a handful is enough.

Yield: 1

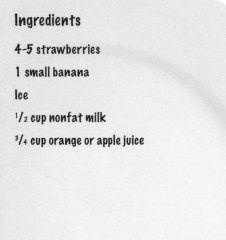

Ingredients

4-5 strawberries

1 small banana

Ice

¹/₂ cup nonfat milk

³/₄ cup orange or apple juice

Banana-berry Smoothie

- On a clean surface, roughly chop the bananas and strawberries.

- Put the ice in a blender and crush it for several seconds on the pulse setting.

- Combine all the ingredients in the blender, and blend on the high-speed setting until smooth.

Calories 225, **Fat** (g) 1, **Carbohydrates** (g) 49, **Protein** (g) 8, **Fiber** (g) 4, **Saturated Fat** (g) 0, **Cholesterol** (mg) 3, **Sodium** (mg) 76

• • • • RECIPE VARIATIONS • • • •

Flax-fortified Smoothie: Add 2 tablespoons of ground flax seed to the fresh fruit, milk, and juice that will go into your smoothie. Flax has been shown to help reduce LDL (bad) cholesterol, and is high in fiber and omega-3 fatty acids, which can play a role in fighting diabetes, inflammation, and boosting immunity.

Wheatgrass-fortified Smoothie: Adding wheatgrass to your smoothie can help boost your energy, as it's packed with enzymes and other nutrients, and contains a complete protein. It's also an excellent source of calcium, iron, magnesium, phosphorus, potassium, sodium, sulfur, cobalt, and zinc.

Adjusting the Consistency

- If you've added flaxseed, spirulina, or wheatgrass to your smoothie and you find that the consistency is too thick, you can thin it out by adding a bit more milk or juice.

- Alternatively, if you find that the consistency of your smoothie is too thin, throw in a bit more banana to thicken it.

Correct Fruit Portions

- For one portion of banana, use one medium-size banana or three-quarters of a large banana.

- For one portion of strawberries, use five strawberries.

EGG MUFFIN SANDWICH

All your favorite breakfast items in a practical, portable sandwich

You might think that a homemade version of a popular fast-food snack is not the best idea for a low-calorie breakfast. But by replacing the bacon with turkey bacon, you can cut your fat intake by half.

If you're a pork lover, you can also opt to make this sandwich with Canadian bacon, which can have as little as one third the calories and one quarter of the saturated fat that regular bacon has. Canadian bacon is made from the loin of the pig, and so it is leaner than regular fatty bacon.

Adding a few greens to your sandwich kicks up its nutritional value and adds an extra touch of color to it.

Yield: 1 sandwich

Ingredients

1 egg

1 whole grain English muffin, halved

2 strips turkey bacon

4-5 leaves baby spinach

¹/₂ teaspoon French mustard

Calories 290, **Fat** (g) 9, **Carbohydrates** (g) 26, **Protein** (g) 27, **Fiber** (g) 2, **Saturated Fat** (g) 2, **Cholesterol** (mg) 262, **Sodium** (mg) 922

Egg Muffin Sandwich

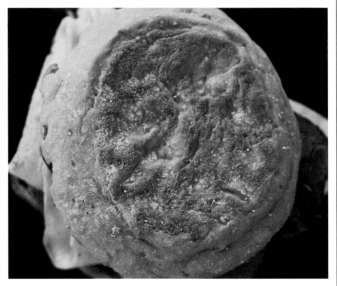

- In a mixing bowl, beat the egg until it's foamy. In a toaster, toast the English muffin halves.

- Spray a large nonstick pan with olive oil and cook bacon over medium-high heat until browned, a few minutes on each side.

- Remove bacon from heat; set aside on a paper towel to absorb excess grease.

- Cook the egg, then remove from heat. Assemble the sandwich with mustard.

· · · · RECIPE VARIATIONS · · · ·

Fried Egg Muffin Sandwich: Make the recipe as described below, except try it with the egg done over easy rather than scrambled. When the sandwich is assembled, the soft yolk will add a whole new flavor dimension to the dish.

Clean Egg Muffin Sandwich: For a less messy version of the Fried Egg Muffin Sandwich, break the yolk of the egg as it fries. The yolk will run into the pan and harden. Turn the egg as you normally would, then assemble the sandwich as described.

Cooking the Egg

Assembling the Sandwich

- Pour the beaten egg into a pan, rotating the pan and scraping back the edges of the egg so that it cooks evenly.

- Once the egg is almost cooked through, fold it in half and turn.

- Fold the egg again, into quarters, and turn again.

- Remove the egg from the heat, and place it on the toasted English muffin.

- Pile the turkey bacon and spinach on top.

- Spread the French mustard on the other half of the English muffin.

- Close the sandwich and serve.

61

HOMEMADE GRANOLA BARS

You'll want to take these bars packed with crunchy nuts and sweet dried berries everywhere

If you can make homemade granola cereal, then you can make a homemade granola bar. The idea is similar, although the execution has a few twists. For starters, the mixture has to be stickier to bake into bar form. Just like when you make granola cereal, you can add whatever nuts or dried fruit you like.

Yield: 12 bars

Ingredients

2 cups rolled oats

¹/₄ cup whole wheat flour

³/₄ cup chopped almonds

³/₄ cup sunflower seeds

1 cup dried cranberries

²/₃ cup brown sugar

¹/₂ cup honey

4 tablespoons vegetable oil

2 teaspoons vanilla extract

¹/₂ teaspoon sea salt

Calories 307, **Fat** (g) 13, **Carbohydrates** (g) 46, **Protein** (g) 6, **Fiber** (g) 4, **Saturated Fat** (g) 1, **Cholesterol** (mg) 0, **Sodium** (mg) 104

Homemade Granola Bars

- In a large mixing bowl, combine all the ingredients. Stir until the mixture is sticking together.

- Line a 9 x 13-inch baking dish with waxed paper and spray with vegetable oil.

- Press the granola mixture into the baking dish and, in an oven preheated to 350°F, bake the granola for about 20 minutes or until golden brown on top.

• • • • RECIPE VARIATIONS • • • •

Nutty Granola: Make the recipe as directed below, except, instead of chopped almonds, use ¾ cup chopped walnuts, pecans, cashews, or peanuts for a variety of new flavors. You can also try a combination of any of these. Nuts are high in unsaturated fats and can promote good cholesterol.

Fruity Granola: Instead of dried cranberries, use 1 cup dried blueberries, dried cherries, semisweet chocolate chips, or a combination of any of the above. Dried fruit can lose some of the nutrients of its fresh counterparts, but gain others. For example, dried blueberries have less vitamin C than fresh, but have been shown to contain up to four times more antioxidants.

Pressing Granola into Dish

- To press the granola into the dish, use a spatula, lightly oiled to keep the mixture from sticking to it.

- Once the granola is done baking, remove the baking dish from the oven. Allow the dish to cool before cutting the granola into bars.

Cutting Granola into Bars

- Using a large, sharp chef's knife, cut the granola into 12 bars.

- Allow the bars to cool completely before serving.

BREAKFAST BURRITO
A delicious breakfast scramble in a soft flour tortilla shell

Burritos are a Tex-Mex favorite. Bigger than their traditional Mexican counterparts, American-style burritos are made up of a large flour tortilla, grilled or steamed to make it more pliable, then filled with any number of meat, rice, beans, and vegetable combinations, and folded into a tight wrap. It's unclear who first thought of stuffing a burrito with a breakfast scramble, but it's a good thing someone did.

For this recipe, simply stuff a tortilla with a quick and easy scramble of eggs, veggies, turkey bacon, and cheese. Then fold it up and take it to go. They can also be made ahead of time and popped in the microwave for 30 seconds in the morning.

Yield: 1

Ingredients

1 egg plus 2 egg whites

1 tablespoon olive oil

$1/4$ cup chopped onion

2 strips turkey bacon, chopped into $1/4$-inch-wide pieces

$1/4$ cup diced bell pepper

$1/4$ cup grated cheddar

1 8-inch soft flour tortilla

Calories 539, **Fat** (g) 33, **Carbohydrates** (g) 25, **Protein** (g) 36, **Fiber** (g) 2, **Saturated Fat** (g) 10, **Cholesterol** (mg) 291, **Sodium** (mg) 911

Breakfast Burrito

- In a mixing bowl, beat egg and egg whites.

- In a large pan over medium-high heat, sauté onion until it's soft and translucent. Remove from pan; set aside.

- Add bacon to the pan and cook for 5 minutes. Return onion to the pan and add the pepper.

- Sauté the veggies with the bacon for a couple more minutes, then add the eggs over top. Sprinkle on the cheese, and cook.

- In another pan, heat up the tortilla. Add scramble to top. Fold and serve.

• • • • RECIPE VARIATIONS • • • •

Veggie Breakfast Burrito: Make this a veggie burrito by swapping out the turkey bacon for ½ cup chopped fresh mushrooms (they will shrink as they cook). Follow the recipe below, except sauté the mushrooms in the pan, then add them to the scramble with the sautéed veggies.

Spicy Breakfast Burrito: Change the flavors in your breakfast burrito by changing the cheese you use. Try ¼ cup of a hearty Monterey Jack or even a spicy Pepper Jack cheese to add a little kick to your burrito.

Making the Scramble

- Stir intermittently as you sauté the veggies and the bacon, then add the beaten eggs over the top.

- Sprinkle on the cheese, and continue to stir intermittently as the eggs cook through.

- The egg mixture should start to gel up.

Preparing the Tortilla

- In another pan, heat the tortilla over medium heat until it browns slightly.

- Alternatively, you can heat your tortilla in the microwave for a few seconds on high.

- Remove the scramble from the pan and scoop it onto the tortilla.

- Fold the tortilla, tucking in the ends and rolling it into a fat cigar. Serve immediately, or wrap it in tinfoil to go.

SIMPLE FRUIT SALAD

Fruit is sweet enough as it is, so this salad doesn't need anything extra

Nothing beats a freshly prepared fruit salad. Sure, canned fruit salads retain some of the nutrients of the original fruits, but if they're packed in syrup, you're consuming extra sugar. Besides, the taste of fresh fruit cannot be replicated in a can.

Many fresh fruit salads call for extra sugar or fruit juice. We like our fruit salad simple—more like a fruit cup.

We've suggested using cantaloupe, honeydew melon, apples, oranges, and grapes, but feel free to add whatever your favorite fruits may be to the mix. Consider color when creating your fruit salad. Not only does a rainbow of fruit colors look pretty, it also ensures an array of nutritional benefits. *Yield: 2*

Ingredients

¹/₄ cantaloupe, cubed

¹/₄ honeydew melon, cubed

¹/₂ apple, chopped

¹/₂ orange, chopped

¹/₂ cup grapes, halved

Simple Fruit Salad

- Forget sugar, extra juices, or flavorings.

- Simply combine the different fruits in a bowl and enjoy.

Calories 148, **Fat** (g) 0.5, **Carbohydrates** (g) 37.5, **Protein** (g) 5, **Fiber** (g) 4, **Saturated Fat** (g) 0, **Cholesterol** (mg) 0, **Sodium** (mg) 41

••••• RECIPE VARIATION •••••

Fruit Salad to Go: If you aren't going to eat your fruit salad right away, you can always preserve the freshness and vibrant colors of the fruit by squeezing the juice of half a lemon over the top. Give the fruit a gentle toss to ensure the lemon juice is well distributed.

ZOOM

Add a dose of iron, calcium, and carbohydrates to your fruit salad with a sprinkle of poppy seeds. Poppies are, of course, known for their opium content, but their seeds are now largely used in baking. Poppy seeds are still said to help regulate sleeplessness. The tiny black seeds also make for a handsome garnish.

Cutting Melon

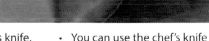

- Using a sharp chef's knife, cut the melon in half.

- Scoop out the seeds, then cut each half in half.

- You can use the chef's knife to cube the melon.

- Alternatively, ball the melon using a melon baller.

Slicing an Apple

- Wash the apple well.

- Using a sharp paring knife, cut it into quarters.

- Cut out the core from each quarter, then cube the apple.

- For extra nutrients, leave the skins on.

BERRIES & COTTAGE CHEESE
Reminiscent of cheesecake, this easy snack hits the spot

The sweetness of fresh berries and the saltiness of cottage cheese are a delightful combination.

The term *cottage cheese* comes from the fact that people first made it at their homes or cottages. Different cultures have different versions of this fresh cheese. It's not only one of the lowest-fat cheeses, it's also high in protein, which is essential to the health of our bones, muscles, cartilage, skin, and blood.

Berries, of course, are easy to find in the supermarket. But nothing tastes better than fruit foraged oneself. To pick a berry, you'll want to look for vibrant color, firm yet squeezable texture, and sweet aroma. Simply take hold of it with your thumb and forefinger, twist, and gently pluck.
Yield: 1

Ingredients

¹/₂ cup low-fat cottage cheese

Handful of fresh blueberries

Handful of fresh raspberries

Berries & Cottage Cheese

- Spoon the cottage cheese into a bowl.
- Sprinkle the berries on top.

Calories 155, **Fat** (g) 2, **Carbohydrates** (g) 21, **Protein** (g) 15, **Fiber** (g) 6, **Saturated Fat** (g) 1, **Cholesterol** (mg) 5, **Sodium** (mg) 460

Honey Sweetened Cottage Cheese: To add a touch of sweetness to this snack, add 1 teaspoon of honey to the cottage cheese and, using a whisk, whip it until it's well incorporated. Honey not only adds another dimension to the flavors of this snack, but also acts as a natural preservative.

Farmer Cheese & Berries: Farmer cheese is a simple, un-aged type of cheese that is made by pressing out much of the moisture from the cottage cheese. Also found in different cultures, farmer cheese is light and spreadable. For this recipe, instead of cottage cheese, spoon ½ of low-fat farmer's cheese into a bowl and cover with two handfuls of your favorite berries for a sweet-savory snack.

Straining Cottage Cheese

- If you find that the brand of cottage cheese you bought is watery, you can drain your portion using a strainer.

- Dump the cottage cheese into your strainer, while holding it over the sink.

- Let all the excess liquid drain out of the strainer before spooning the cottage cheese into the bowl.

Handful of Berries

- Make sure your berries are fresh.

- Blueberries should be dark blue in color and snappy in texture, and anywhere from sweet to tart in the mouth.

- Raspberries, which are delicate and easily damaged, should be bright red and firm.

MELON & MINT

This simple snack is cooling, refreshing, and hydrating

In Chinese medicine, melon is considered a cooling food. Because it's made of so much water, it definitely can work to hydrate you. More than just a refreshing snack, watermelon is packed with antioxidants, as well as with the cancer-fighting carotenoid lycopene, which is also found in tomatoes. Watermelon's vitamin C and beta-carotene help prevent heart disease and can alleviate symptoms of asthma.

Cantaloupe is an excellent source of vitamin A. This nutrient,

along with beta-carotene, which is found in many orange fruits and vegetables, not only promotes eye health, but can also prevent certain lung diseases. Mint not only makes this snack refreshing, but, like other herbs, contains cancer-fighting agents. It's also known for soothing the belly.

Yield: 1

Ingredients

¹/₂ cantaloupe, cubed or balled

¹/₄ small watermelon, cubed or balled

¹/₄ cup chopped fresh mint

Juice of ¹/₂ lime

Melon & Mint

- Toss the melon with the mint and lime juice in a bowl.

- Garnish with a sprig of mint and serve.

Calories 145, **Fat** (g) 1, **Carbohydrates** (g) 36, **Protein** (g) 3, **Fiber** (g) 3, **Saturated Fat** (g) 0, **Cholesterol** (mg) 0, **Sodium** (mg) 46

• • • • RECIPE VARIATIONS • • • •

Melon & Feta Salad: For a touch of savory—not to mention an extra protein kick—add 2 ounces of feta to your salad. Prepare the melon as described below, then crumble the feta on top of the melon and toss with the other ingredients.

Melon & Mint with a Kick: Speaking of kicking up your snack, try this version for grownups only. Prepare the melon and mint as described below, except add one ounce of cognac or some other brandy to the mix and toss with the other ingredients. Best to enjoy this version of the snack on a weekend afternoon or evening.

Cutting Watermelon

- Cutting watermelon can be a daunting task because they are such big, heavy fruits with tough rinds.

- Start by rinsing the rind. Using a sharp chef's knife, cut the ends of the melon off.

- Stand the melon on end, then slice down the middle.

- Cut each half into wedges. Using a paring knife, remove the flesh from the rind on each wedge. Cube the flesh.

Chopping Mint

- Soak the mint in a cold-water bath until the dirt sinks to the bottom.

- Repeat if necessary, then pat the mint dry.

- Remove the leaves from the stems. Pile them together on a cutting board.

- Rock the blade of a sharp chef's knife back and forth over the pile of mint leaves. As they scatter, gather them together again. Repeat until the mint is finely chopped.

APPLES & CINNAMON DIP

With the age-old combo of apples and cinnamon, you can't go wrong

Reminiscent of apple pie, this flavor combination is familiar and comforting. But you can also change up the recipe with other favorite flavor combinations.

This recipe calls for Greek-style yogurt, which is thicker and creamier than the American kind. It contains less sugar than many American yogurts, which makes it easy to use in both sweet and savory snacks. Greek-style yogurt also contains more protein than American-style yogurt. Studies have shown that eating just half a teaspoon daily of cinnamon can help lower bad cholesterol, relieve arthritis pain, and kill food borne bacteria.

Yield: 1

Ingredients

¹/₂ cup plain nonfat Greek yogurt

¹/₂ teaspoon vanilla extract

¹/₂ teaspoon cinnamon

1 teaspoon brown sugar

1 apple

Apples & Cinnamon Dip

- In a bowl, combine the yogurt, vanilla extract, cinnamon, and brown sugar, and whip together.

- Cut the apple into wedges and dip.

Calories 220, **Fat** (g) 2, **Carbohydrates** (g) 47, **Protein** (g) 6, **Fiber** (g) 3, **Saturated Fat** (g) 1, **Cholesterol** (mg) 5, **Sodium** (mg) 74

Peaches & Creamy Yogurt Dip: Prepare the snack as described below, except instead of cinnamon and vanilla, add 1 teaspoon of honey to the yogurt, then whip the two together until well incorporated. Serve it with wedges of fresh peach for a peaches and cream effect.

Strawberries and Chocolate Yogurt Dip: Prepare the snack as described below, except instead of cinnamon and vanilla, stir 1 tablespoon of chocolate powder or fat-free chocolate syrup into the yogurt. Serve it with strawberries for a chocolate-covered strawberries effect.

Whipping the Ingredients

- Whip up the yogurt in a bowl using a whisk.

- Because Greek yogurt is already so thick and creamy, you won't have to work too hard.

- Hold the bowl against your body with one hand and whisk briskly with the other for maximum results.

Coring the Apple

- Use a metal apple corer to core the apple.

- Alternatively, you can use a potato peeler. Cut the apple in half, then hold one half in your palm as you drive the sharp tip of the peeler into the core to dig it out.

SPICY HOT CHOCOLATE
Sometimes the best snack is a nice hot drink

A touch of spice makes this hot chocolate more than just a sweet treat. Cayenne pepper adds a depth of flavor to chocolate—hey, Mexicans have been adding chiles to their chocolate for centuries! It also fortifies the hot chocolate with the healing properties of this hot red spice. The powder made from hot capsicum peppers is said to promote healthy circulation and digestion.

And, seeing as the chocolate syrup in this snack has no fat at all, the only real calories are coming from the milk. We chose to use 2 percent instead of skim milk for this recipe for the extra protein and calcium that it contains.
Yield: 1 cup

Ingredients

8 ounces low-fat (2 percent) milk

3 tablespoons nonfat chocolate syrup

Pinch of cayenne pepper

Spicy Hot Chocolate

- In a saucepan over medium heat, warm the milk.

- Pour the syrup into a mug, then stir in the milk and cayenne pepper.

Calories 254, **Fat** (g) 1, **Carbohydrates** (g) 50, **Protein** (g) 10, **Fiber** (g) 2, **Saturated Fat** (g) 1, **Cholesterol** (mg) 5, **Sodium** (mg) 172

Coffee has almost no calories whatsoever. And, while you should limit your intake of caffeine and diuretics, drinking a moderate amount of coffee every day has not been shown to be harmful. Add a shot of strong coffee or espresso to this hot chocolate and you've made yourself a gourmet-style cafe drink. Call it a Mexican mochaccino!

• • • • RECIPE VARIATION • • • •

Mint-infused Hot Chocolate: Mint brightens the taste of chocolate—just ask anyone whose favorite ice cream flavor is chocolate mint. To add zing to your hot chocolate, prepare it as described below, except instead of adding a pinch of cayenne pepper, stir in an ounce of strong mint green tea. Garnish with a fresh sprig of mint.

Heating Milk

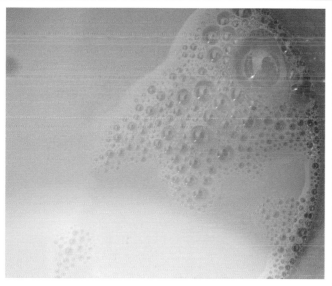

- Warm the milk over medium heat to avoid burning it.
- If you have a handheld milk frother, you may also want to froth the milk.

A Pinch of Cayenne

- To add a pinch of cayenne pepper, use your thumb, index finger, and middle finger to grab the powder.
- To add a small pinch of cayenne pepper, use just your thumb and index finger.

FIGS & HONEY

Feel like Greek royalty with this simple snack

Figs and honey are two foods traditionally associated with luxury and prosperity. Figs are in season at the end of the summer but are enjoyed dried year-round. An excellent source of dietary fiber, they are said to help with weight management. Figs are delicious raw, but they can also be roasted.

Feel like a Greek god or goddess with this simple combination of figs and honey—both native to ancient Greece, and both representing bounty and indulgence. Honey has antibacterial, antiviral and antifungal properties, and boasts the ability to fight infection and boost immunity. The two together feel like an extravagant treat, but are in fact a healthful snack.

Yield: 1

Ingredients

6 medium fresh figs, halved

2 tablespoons honey

Figs & Honey

- Cut off the ends of the figs, and slice them in half.
- Drizzle the honey over the figs and serve.

Calories 414, **Fat** (g) 1, **Carbohydrates** (g) 109, **Protein** (g) 2, **Fiber** (g) 9, **Saturated Fat** (g) 0, **Cholesterol** (mg) 0, **Sodium** (mg) 6

Honey-roasted Figs: To make honey-roasted figs, cut off the ends of the figs, then slice them in half. Place them cut side up in a baking dish and drizzle them with honey. Roast them at 350°F for 12–15 minutes.

Goat Cheese Figs: Prepare the recipe as directed. However, place a dab of goat cheese—no more than ¼ teaspoon—on each fig before you drizzle it with honey. You can do this for raw figs or roasted figs.

Picking Figs

- Figs come in a variety of colors, from yellow and brown to purple, red, and black.

- Make sure to select figs that are firm with no bruises, yet still dent if you press the skin.

- Smell them: the figs should be fragrant.

Drizzling the Honey

- You can use honey from a squeeze bottle, although it's a good idea to measure it using a spoon or measuring tool before drizzling.

- Honey, while delicious and nutritious, is high in calories and should be used sparingly.

CELERY & PEANUT BUTTER

Make your own peanut butter for this classic snack

This is the kind of snack your mom prepared for you when you came home from school. But homemade peanut butter makes these celery sticks sing.

Add raisins to your peanut butter–covered celery stalks for a little snack your mom might have called "Ants on a Log." Raisins add a dose of antioxidants and a shot of color to the snack.

This recipe calls for unsalted raw peanuts. Be sure not to use salted peanuts, as you will be adding salt. Using honey means not only opting for a natural sweetener but also incorporating a natural preservative into the peanut butter. Store it in a sealable plastic container to use as needed.

Yield: 4 servings (2 stalks per serving)

Ingredients

¹/₂ cup unsalted peanuts

1 tablespoon vegetable oil

¹/₂ tablespoon honey

Pinch of sea salt

8 celery stalks

Celery & Peanut Butter

- Combine the peanuts, vegetable oil, honey, and sea salt in a blender or food processor, and blend until smooth.

- Spread 1 tablespoon of the peanut butter on each celery stalk.

Calories 153, **Fat** (g) 13, **Carbohydrates** (g) 7, **Protein** (g) 5, **Fiber** (g) 3, **Saturated Fat** (g) 2, **Cholesterol** (mg) 0, **Sodium** (mg) 106

Almond Butter: Instead of peanut butter, make almond butter. Spread out ½ cup raw almonds on a cookie sheet and toast them for 10 minutes or so in an oven preheated to 350°F. Add them to the blender or food processor with the other ingredients and blend until smooth.

Ants on a Log: You're all grown up but that doesn't mean you still can't have fun with food. For an extra shot of antioxidants and a splash of color, prepare your snack as described below, then take ¼ cup of raisins or dried cranberries and space them out evenly along the celery stick.

Blending the Ingredients

- Blend the ingredients on high speed.

- If necessary, use a spatula to scrape the splatter on the sides of the blender container back down for more blending.

Spreading the Peanut Butter

- Spread just 1 tablespoon of peanut butter on each celery stalk.

- To add color and fiber to the snack, dot the length of the celery stalk with raisins. You might remember your mom calling this ants on a log!

HARD-BOILED EGG

Perfect for picnics and snack breaks, a hard-boiled egg can't be beat!

They might announce themselves with a pungent odor, but hard-boiled eggs are ideal low-calorie, high-protein snacks. Making the perfect hard-boiled egg is not as easy or obvious as it may seem. The cooking time is precise—after all, there's nothing worse than an overdone egg.

Eggs get a bad rap for their fat and cholesterol content, but much of the fat in eggs is unsaturated and studies have shown that the bad (LDL) cholesterol in eggs may be offset by its good (HDL) cholesterol content. Eggs also boast a slew of nutritional benefits, including six grams of high-quality protein per egg, and all nine essential amino acids.

Yield: 1

Ingredients

2 eggs

Sea salt and freshly ground pepper, to taste

Hard-boiled Egg

- Place the eggs in a saucepan and cover with cold water.

- Cover the pot and bring it to a boil over high heat.

- Once the first bubbles appear, turn the heat off.

- Let the pot stand for 8–12 minutes. Drain eggs, and let them stand for another 10–12 minutes before peeling, seasoning, and eating.

Calories 156, **Fat** (g) 10, **Carbohydrates** (g) 2, **Protein** (g) 12, **Fiber** (g) 0, **Saturated Fat** (g) 4, **Cholesterol** (mg) 424, **Sodium** (mg) 744

Fancy Hard-boiled Eggs: Dress up your hard-boiled egg with slivers of red bell pepper and a sprinkle of black olives. Slice the egg in half lengthwise and place a few slivers of red bell pepper on each half, then arrange pitted and sliced black olives on top.

Deli Hard-boiled Eggs: Slice the egg lengthwise and arrange a few sliced gherkin pickles over the yolk. Add a dab of horseradish on top of the pickles.

Salted Hard-boiled Eggs: Have fun with salt. If you're just salting your hard-boiled egg, try a pinch of black Cyprus or red lava sea salt.

Cooling in Ice Bath

- If you're in a hurry, you can also transfer the eggs to an ice bath to cool them.

- This will also ensure that they stop cooking inside the shell.

- Using a large spoon, carefully transfer the eggs to a bowl filled with ice and water.

- Let them sit there for 5 minutes.

Peeling an Egg

- Stand the egg upright on a hard surface and tap it firmly.

- Turn it over and do the same with the other end.

- Turn the egg on its side and roll it on a hard surface, pressing down.

- Submerge the egg in a warm water bath and the shell will just slip off.

MORNING SNACKS TO GO

APPLES & CHEESE

Has there ever been a better combo than sweet apples and savory cheese?

Sweet and salty are made to go together. Apples and cheese can be a simple, fun snack for you and the kids or sophisticated finger food just for adults. The flavor combinations are endless: a Red Delicious with sharp cheddar, a Granny Smith with a soft Brie, an Asian pear with a sheep's-milk Manchego. Just as you can pair wine with cheese, you can find the

perfect apple to go with your favorite *fromage*.

Cheese and apple platters are also pretty to look at. If you're having friends over, assemble a cheese and apple plate for everyone to nibble on. Your friends will appreciate this tasty, light snack, and you can indulge, guilt-free, too.
Yield: 1

Ingredients

1 apple

1 ounce sharp cheddar cheese

Apples & Cheese

- Halve and core the apple.

- Slice it into wedges.

- Using a cheese knife or any small sharp knife, cut the cheese into slices or wedges, depending on its shape.

Calories 224, **Fat** (g) 10, **Carbohydrates** (g) 30, **Protein** (g) 8, **Fiber** (g) 5, **Saturated Fat** (g) 6, **Cholesterol** (mg) 30, **Sodium** (mg) 178

Cheese-stuffed Apples: Why not stuff your apples with cheese? In a mixing bowl, combine 1 cup of low-fat cottage cheese with 1 ounce of grated sharp cheddar (or whatever hard cheese you like). Whip the two together until well incorporated. Halve your apple and, using a melon baller, scoop out the core, making a little bowl out of the apple. Spoon the cheese mixture into the bowl, and enjoy.

Grilled (Apple &) Cheese Sandwich: Take 2 slices of whole wheat bread, and add a few slices of cheddar on one of them. Toast them in the oven at 250ºF for 10 minutes until the cheese begins to bubble. Remove them from the oven, add several slices of green apple over the cheese and close the sandwich for a sweet and savory snack.

Slicing Cheese

- Use a cheese knife, especially when cutting round cheeses.

- With blocks of cheese, you can use a small sharp knife.

- If using a round cheese, cut out a narrow wedge, no more than 1 inch thick. Don't avoid the rind.

- If using a block of cheese, cut ¼-inch-thick slices.

Wrapping Your Snack

- Wrap up your cheese and apple slices separately in plastic wrap to enjoy on the go.

- Some experts say you should first wrap the cheese in wax paper, then wrap the whole in plastic to avoid having chemicals from the plastic leak into the cheese, affecting its taste and composition.

DRIED FRUIT SALAD
Like a fruit salad concentrate, mixed dried fruits are good to go

Dried fruits are like nature's little candy pieces. The sugars and other nutrients contained in the fruits get concentrated when the fruit is dried. While some of the nutrients are lost during the drying process, studies have shown that certain dried fruits have four times the antioxidants of their fresh equivalents.

You can use any combination of dried apples, apricots, cranberries, blueberries, bananas, mango, cherries, and pineapple in your dried fruit salad. To liven it up, try reconstituting the fruit. You can also combine the dried fruit with nuts, an easy combination. The protein from the nuts is the perfect companion for the carbohydrate-packed dried fruit.

Yield: 2

Ingredients

¹/₄ cup dried apples

¹/₄ cup dried apricots

¹/₄ cup dried cranberries

¹/₄ cup dried mango

Dried Fruit Salad

- Combine ingredients in a bowl or sandwich bag, and serve.

Calories 189, **Fat** (g) 0, **Carbohydrates** (g) 49, **Protein** (g) 1, **Fiber** (g) 4, **Saturated Fat** (g) 0, **Cholesterol** (mg) 0, **Sodium** (mg) 22

Reconstituted Dried Fruit Salad: Combine all the dried fruits in a saucepan with a cinnamon stick and a couple of cloves. Pour ½ cup of apple or orange juice over the dried fruits, and bring to a boil. Reduce the heat and allow the mixture to simmer for 15 minutes or so. Allow the fruit to cool before serving on its own or over plain nonfat Greek yogurt.

Dried Fruit & Nuts: Serve your dried fruit salad with mixed nuts, or alternatively, combine the two in a single bowl. Raw almonds, hazelnuts, and cashews will add the perfect amount of savory to this otherwise sweet snack.

Measuring Dried Fruit

- If you need to measure a quarter cup of a solid food, you can eyeball it.

- Make a fist: That's a cup. Now, release your pinky, ring, and middle fingers.

- Your clenched index finger and thumb are equivalent to the size of ¼ cup of dried fruit.

Dried Fruit to Go

- Take your dried fruit salad to go in a sandwich bag, sealable plastic container, or even a small cookie tin.

MORNING SNACKS TO GO

FRESH FRUIT SORBET

This simple sorbet will not only tide you over but refresh you, too

Peaches may sound sweet, but these fuzzy little fruits are packed with beta-carotene, potassium, and heart-disease-preventing lycopene, among other nutrients.

Buy frozen peaches or freeze your own for this cool, refreshing snack. The honey and lemon act as natural preservatives, so you can feel free to make enough to store.

Double or even quadruple this recipe if you like, but be sure to store each portion in individual containers, as you need to thaw out the sorbet for ten minutes before serving. You should never thaw then re-freeze any type of dish, as it can lead to food contamination and an overall disintegration of foodstuffs.

Yield: 1

Ingredients

4 ounces frozen peaches

2 tablespoons honey

Juice of ¼ lemon

Pinch of salt

Calories 220, **Fat** (g) 0, **Carbohydrates** (g) 58, **Protein** (g) 1, **Fiber** (g) 2, **Saturated Fat** (g) 0, **Cholesterol** (mg) 0, **Sodium** (mg) 163

Fresh Fruit Sorbet

- Combine the ingredients in a blender and blend on high speed. Serve immediately or freeze for later.

- If you freeze the sorbet, let it thaw for 10 minutes before serving.

- Add extra ice to the blender to turn your sorbet into a sippable granita.

Peaches and Cream: Turn this fresh peach sorbet into a version of peaches and cream. Whip together ¼ cup of plain nonfat Greek yogurt with a dash of vanilla extract and a pinch of brown sugar. Serve your sorbet with a dollop on top.

Peaches & Store-bought Cream: We are fans of making meals and snacks from scratch, using fresh ingredients and whole foods. But sometimes, certain processed foods just can't be replicated. Add a dollop of any fat-free whipped topping to your sorbet for an extra special treat.

Freezing Fresh Peaches

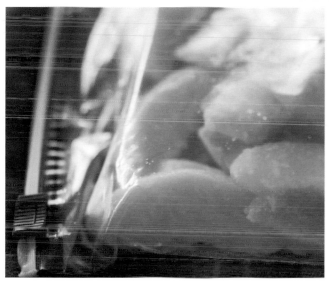

Blending the Ingredients

- Choose fresh, ripe (but not overripe) peaches.

- To peel the peaches, cut an X into each one, then dip them in a pot of boiling water for about 30 seconds, then immediately transfer them to an ice bath for a few minutes. The skins should slip right off.

- Place the peaches in a large food storage bag and cover with apple juice.

- Alternatively, cover the peaches with simple syrup, which is a combination of equal parts sugar (or Splenda) and water, boiled until the sugar is dissolved and the liquid is syrupy.

- Blend the sorbet ingredients on high speed.

- If you add extra ice to the recipe to make your sorbet into more of a granita, blend it on the pulse setting.

APPLESAUCE & GRAHAM CRACKERS

Making your own applesauce is as easy as, well, pie (actually, it's much easier!)

It was one of the first foods you ever ate, and applesauce is still a treat. Packed with fiber, filled with nutrients, and great for digestion, apples also promote tooth and gum health. You can make this applesauce with any type of apple, but sweet, crisp, aromatic varieties, such as Gala and Fuji apples, work best.

Sweetened with maple syrup, this applesauce is enriched with antioxidants and an extra dose of zinc. The nutrients in top-grade maple syrup have been shown to boost the immune system and promote a healthy heart. Because maple syrup is unrefined, you don't need as much of it as you would regular sugar. *Yield: 2 servings*

Applesauce & Graham Crackers

Ingredients

4 apples, peeled, cored, and sliced

2 tablespoons maple syrup

Pinch of cinnamon

Graham crackers

- Place the apples in a sauce-pan and cover with water.

- Cook over low heat for 20 minutes or until apples become soft and the water is absorbed.

- Add the maple syrup and cinnamon, stirring well.

- Serve with a couple graham crackers.

Calories 176, **Fat** (g) 0, **Carbohydrates** (g) 46, **Protein** (g) 1, **Fiber** (g) 3, **Saturated Fat** (g) 0, **Cholesterol** (mg) 0, **Sodium** (mg) 2

A Little Applesauce with Your Cake: Instead of serving it with graham crackers, dip biscotti, or even a wedge of angel food cake, in your applesauce.. The tang of the apples will cut the sweetness of the cake or cookie.

Frozen Applesauce Sandwich: In warm weather, use your applesauce to make a frozen treat. Whip together one part applesauce and two parts fat-free whipped topping. Spread a thick layer on a graham cracker. Top it with another graham cracker and freeze overnight.

Peeling Apples

Preparing to Serve

- Start by coring the apple with a metal apple corer.

- You can use the hole to help you hold on to the apple as you peel.

- Use a vegetable peeler to remove the skin on one side, then the other.

- If using a paring knife, apply it at an angle as you work it around the apple, removing the skin in strips.

- Adjust the thickness of the sauce with water, if necessary.

- Allow the applesauce to cool before serving with graham crackers.

SPINACH & FETA QUICHE

Use a frozen piecrust or make your own for this savory quiche

Traditional quiches call for heavy cream, but you can turn out light, satisfying versions of the dish made with skim milk instead.

The beauty of a quiche is that you can toss anything into it, really. All you need is a piecrust, some eggs, milk, and whatever meat, veggies, or cheese you have lying around.

We've suggested using skim milk for this quiche. Should you wish to make your version a little fluffier, go for a 2 percent reduced fat milk. It will add a few more calories to the dish, but also add extra protein and calcium.

Yield: 6 servings

Ingredients

1 tablespoon olive oil

1/2 yellow onion, diced small

1 clove garlic, minced

1 cup frozen spinach

2 eggs plus 3 egg whites

1/4 cup nonfat milk

1/2 cup crumbled feta

2 tablespoons finely chopped parsley

1 9-inch piecrust

Calories 195, **Fat** (g) 13, **Carbohydrates** (g) 13, **Protein** (g) 7, **Fiber** (g) 1, **Saturated Fat** (g) 4, **Cholesterol** (mg) 47, **Sodium** (mg) 339

Spinach & Feta Quiche

- In a sauté pan over medium-high heat, sauté onion in oil until soft and translucent. Add garlic and spinach; cook for another couple of minutes. Remove mixture from the pan.

- In a large mixing bowl, whisk eggs, egg whites, and milk together until foamy.

- Add the spinach mixture, as well as the feta and parsley, to the egg mixture, and stir everything together thoroughly.

- Pour into baked piecrust. Bake in a 350°F preheated oven for 30 minutes or until well set.

Quiche Lorraine: Instead of using spinach and feta, try a traditional quiche lorraine, with grated Gruyère and small cubes of cooked ham. Add 1 cup of cubed ham and ½ cup of grated Gruyère to your egg mixture for a traditional French quiche.

Dinner Leftovers Quiche: Have leftover chicken and broccoli from dinner last night? Chop them up and toss roughly 1 cup of each into your egg mixture for a hearty quiche. Leftover sausage, roasted vegetables, salmon, zucchini, and tomatoes also work—or any combination of the above.

Preparing the Filling

- When cooking the vegetables, you may have to add a few drops of water to revive the spinach.

- Once the eggs and milk are whisked together, add the spinach mixture and whisk thoroughly.

Baking and Using Piecrust

- Whether using your own homemade piecrust or a store-bought frozen one, if the crust is not yet cooked, you'll want to prebake it.

- Place pie weights on the crust (in its pie tin) so that it doesn't fluff up. You can also use paper coffee filters filled with beans.

- Bake the piecrust at 400°F for 20 minutes to prebake it. Remove it from the oven and allow it to cool for a few minutes.

- Then pour the filling mixture into the piecrust.

LEISURELY LUNCH

TURKEY BURGERS

Make these turkey burgers indoors or on the grill out back

Burgers may be the most quintessentially American food out there. But burgers don't have to be loaded with fat and calories. Use lean meat, whole wheat buns, and plenty of fresh fixings for a lighter version of America's favorite sandwich.

Turkey burgers can be a healthy alternative to beef burgers, but you have to read the label. The meat must be specified as "lean ground turkey breast"; otherwise, it might contain skin and dark meat, which can be higher in fat than lean ground beef.

If you have an outdoor grill, make these outside with the family. Lay out a table of fixings: lettuce, tomato, diced onion, sliced American cheese, mustard, relish, and low-fat mayo, so people can serve themselves.

Yield: 6 burgers

KNACK CALORIE COUNTER COOKBOOK

Ingredients

1 pound lean ground turkey breast

½ red onion, finely chopped

3 cloves garlic, minced

1 egg white

¼ cup finely chopped fresh parsley

Sea salt and freshly ground pepper, to taste

6 English muffins

1 teaspoon Dijon mustard, for garnish

Lettuce, for garnish

Tomato slices, for garnish

Calories 253, **Fat** (g) 8, **Carbohydrates** (g) 27, **Protein** (g) 18, **Fiber** (g) 2, **Saturated Fat** (g) 3, **Cholesterol** (mg) 61, **Sodium** (mg) 529

Turkey Burgers

- In a large mixing bowl, combine all the ingredients (except for English muffins and garnishes); using your hands works best.

- Divide the meat into 6 parts and shape into round patties.

- Spray a nonstick pan with olive oil and, over medium-high heat, cook the burgers for a few minutes on each side until well done. (Or use a grill instead.)

- Lightly toast the English muffins. Place a patty on each muffin and garnish with Dijon mustard, lettuce, and tomato.

• • • • RECIPE VARIATIONS • • • •

Beef Burgers: Make the recipe as directed below, except substitute 1 pound ground beef for the ground turkey breast. Again, reading the label is important. Make sure you get lean ground beef, such as ground sirloin, raised without hormones or antibiotics.

Spicy Turkey Burgers: Kick up your burgers with a little spice. Follow the recipe below, but add 2 tablespoons canned chipotle chiles in adobo sauce to your meat mixture. Chipotle chiles are dried, smoked jalapenos. They often come canned in adobo, a tomato-based sauce with spices, vinegar, garlic, onions and sometimes other chiles.

Forming Patties

- Take a portion of meat and roll it into a sphere between your palms.

- Using your palms, flatten the patty to 1 or 1½ inches thick.

Cooking Burgers

- Lay the burger on a well-oiled cooking surface, either in a pan or on a grill.

- Allow the burgers to cook on each side for 8–10 minutes, depending on how well done you want them.

- Turn your burger just once. Avoid flattening it with a spatula—this squeezes out all the juices.

- If adding cheese to your burger, do so as it's cooking on the second side, about 2–3 minutes before it's done.

QUINOA, BEET, & FETA SALAD
Not quite a grain, quinoa is a protein-packed superfood

Quinoa often gets lobbed in with other grains like couscous and millet, but is not, in fact, a grain at all. Quinoa is a grain-like plant grown primarily for its seeds. It's one of the few foods that deliver a complete protein, meaning that it contains all nine essential amino acids necessary to build muscle in the body. Quinoa is also an excellent source of fiber, magnesium (which is good for your cardiovascular health), and copper and iron (which have been shown, among their other

benefits, to prevent migraines). You can find black, red, and the traditional "white" (actually, more of a wheat color) varieties. Try different types to create different looks for this dish. *Yield: 2 servings*

Ingredients

2 cups water

1 cup uncooked red quinoa

2 tablespoons pine nuts

1/2 red onion, diced small

2 beets, cooked and julienned

1/4 cup dried cranberries

1/4 cup crumbled feta

1/4 cup finely chopped cilantro

3 tablespoons vinaigrette (recipe follows)

For the vinaigrette:

1/2 cup olive oil	1 teaspoon fresh ginger, peeled
1/2 small beet, cooked	1/2 teaspoon salt
1/4 cup apple cider vinegar	1/4 teaspoon sweet paprika
3 cloves garlic	1/4 teaspoon cayenne pepper

Calories 574, **Fat** (g) 20, **Carbohydrates** (g) 87, **Protein** (g) 16, **Fiber** (g) 9, **Saturated Fat** (g) 5, **Cholesterol** (mg) 17, **Sodium** (mg) 561

Quinoa, Beet, & Feta Salad

- For the vinaigrette:

- Toss all the ingredients into a blender and liquefy.

- For the salad:

- In a small pot over high heat, bring the water and quinoa to a boil.

- Cook for about 10 minutes, until the water is absorbed.

- Drain the quinoa and rinse it under cold water.

- Toast the pine nuts. Combine quinoa and pine nuts with the other ingredients in a salad bowl, add vinaigrette, and serve.

Quinoa Salad with Toasted Almonds: Instead of toasting pine nuts for this salad, try toasting almond slivers. The process is the same: spray or brush the nuts with olive oil and toast in the oven at 350°F for 10 minutes.

Couscous and Feta Salad: Instead of using quinoa, make this salad using any number of grains or beans, including lentils, couscous, and even wild rice. For couscous, use two parts water or vegetable stock to one part couscous. Bring the water or stock to a boil, add the dried couscous, then remove from heat and let sit, covered, for 5 minutes or so until the liquid is entirely absorbed.

Toasting Pine Nuts

- Spread out the pine nuts on a nonstick cookie sheet and spray them with olive oil.
- In an oven preheated to 350°F, toast the pine nuts for 10–15 minutes or until lightly browned, turning them once.

Combining Ingredients

- In a large salad bowl, combine the quinoa, pine nuts, onion, beets, dried cranberries, feta, and cilantro.
- Toss the salad with the vinaigrette and serve at room temperature.

LEISURELY LUNCH

95

LEMON CHICKEN BREAST SALAD

Marinated chicken breast makes this salad a protein-rich lunch

Still-warm lemon-marinated chicken breast is the key to this simple salad. Make sure your breast is skinless, free-range, and antibiotic-free to avoid consuming any excess fat, unwanted chemicals, or hormones.

When preparing chicken, it's important to take precautions to ensure food safety. Rinsing your raw chicken breast under cold water, then patting it dry using a paper towel is a good way to avoid food borne illnesses. But meats are not the only foods that can become contaminated. It's important to wash all vegetables and leafy greens. Use a salad spinner to wash the lettuce or simply rinse it under cold water and pat it dry. And, just to be safe, wash it twice.

Yield: 2 servings

KNACK CALORIE COUNTER COOKBOOK

Ingredients

¹/₄ cup lemon juice

3 tablespoons olive oil

4 ounces free-range antibiotic-free chicken breast

Sea salt and freshly ground pepper, to taste

¹/₂ cucumber

¹/₂ yellow bell pepper

¹/₂ cup cherry tomatoes

¹/₂ head romaine lettuce

3 tablespoons vinaigrette (recipe follows)

Fresh parsley, finely chopped (keep one sprig whole for garnish)

For the vinaigrette:

¹/₂ cup olive oil	¹/₄ cup lemon juice
¹/₄ cup red wine vinegar	1 tablespoon French mustard

Calories 467, **Fat** (g) 30, **Carbohydrates** (g) 19, **Protein** (g) 34, **Fiber** (g) 5, **Saturated Fat** (g) 5, **Cholesterol** (mg) 83, **Sodium** (mg) 466

Lemon Chicken Breast Salad

- For the vinaigrette: Combine ingredients in a sealable container and shake well.

- For the salad: Combine lemon juice and olive oil in a shallow bowl; whisk well.

- Rinse and pat dry chicken breast. Salt and pepper it before placing in marinade.

- Cover; let sit in the fridge 20 minutes or longer.

- Cut cucumber, pepper, tomatoes, and lettuce into bite size pieces.

- Sear; cook chicken. Slice. Assemble salad; top with vinaigrette and parsley.

Lemon Chicken on Swiss Chard: The easiest way to change up this salad is to change the lettuce used. Try replacing the romaine with 2 cups of bitter, savory Swiss chard for a healthy dose of calcium, iron, and vitamin K, plus fiber.

Garlic Marinade: Instead of a lemon marinade, whip up an easy garlic marinade. Toss 3 cloves of garlic, ¼ cup olive oil, 2 tablespoons of soy sauce, and 1 tablespoon of white vinegar into a blender and liquefy. Place your chicken breast in a bowl with this mixture, cover it, and let it sit in the fridge for 20 minutes or longer.

Cooking Chicken Breast

- Spray a pan or cast-iron skillet with olive oil and, over high heat, sear the chicken breast for 3–4 minutes on each side.

- Remove the chicken from heat and place it in an oven preheated to 350°F, for 12–15 minutes or until cooked through.

- Cast-iron is oven-friendly, but if your pan is not, transfer the chicken to a baking dish.

Assembling the Salad

- After removing chicken from the oven, let it cool for 5–10 minutes.

- Slice the breast on an angle into ¾-inch slices.

- In a salad bowl, combine the lettuce, tomatoes, bell pepper, and cucumber, and toss with the vinaigrette and parsley.

- Arrange the chicken slices over top and finish with a sprig of parsley.

LEISURELY LUNCH

FISH TACOS

These California-style tacos are sure to win you and your family over

This California favorite makes for a fresh and delicious lunch option. We recommend using tilapia. It's a lower-fat fish with a delicate flavor, and is one of the best species of fish to eat from an environmental perspective, as U.S.-farmed tilapia does not involve overharvesting or a reduction in biodiversity.

Because tilapia is a vegetarian species of fish—unlike other oily fish—it subsists on seaweed rather than other smaller fish species and has lower levels of mercury than other species. Tilapia is also lower in fat than other popular kinds of fish, such as salmon.

Its light texture and flavor make it ideal for battering, and cooking with other subtle flavors.

Yield: 1

Ingredients

¹/₂ cup all-purpose flour

Sea salt and cayenne pepper, to taste

2 4-ounce tilapia fillets

1 egg white

1 squeeze of lime juice

2 4-inch flour tortillas

¹/₄ cup shredded iceberg lettuce or cabbage

Guacamole (recipe follows)

Cilantro sprigs, for garnish

For the guacamole:

1 ripe avocado

1 plum tomato, diced small

¹/₂ red onion, diced small

¹/₄ cup finely chopped cilantro

1 tablespoon fresh lemon juice

Sea salt and freshly ground pepper, to taste

Calories 579, **Fat** (g) 19, **Carbohydrates** (g) 66, **Protein** (g) 40, **Fiber** (g) 13, **Saturated Fat** (g) 3, **Cholesterol** (mg) 95, **Sodium** (mg) 749

Fish Tacos

- In a small bowl, combine the flour with the salt and cayenne pepper.

- Brush each fillet with egg white, then lightly dredge it in the seasoned flour.

- Spray a pan with olive oil and place the fillets in the pan over medium heat.

- Cook for a few minutes on each side.

- Squirt the fish with a squeeze of lime juice. In a bowl, break it up.

- Assemble tacos. Top with lettuce, guacamole, and cilantro.

• • • • RECIPE VARIATIONS • • • •

Catfish Tacos: Try this recipe using catfish, another lower-fat fish that, when farmed, does not harm the environment. Take 2 4-ounce fillets of catfish, then batter and lightly fry it as is described below. Catfish is heartier and flakier in texture than tilapia.

Mango Salsa: Instead of guacamole, make an easy mango salsa. Dice 1 ripe mango and 1 small red onion, and toss them together with the juice of 1 lime, 1 tablespoon of red wine vinegar, and 1 tablespoon of finely chopped fresh cilantro. Allow the mixture to sit covered in the fridge for 20 minutes or longer.

Skinning and Dredging Fish

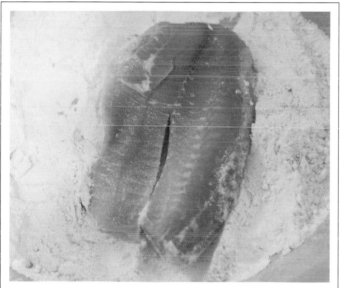

- If your fillet still has the skin on, take a sharp pointed knife and place it at an angle at the tip of the fillet.

- Place your hand on the fillet to secure it (but not too hard, to avoid bruising it) and gently push the knife along the skin to separate it from the flesh.

- To dredge the fish, take each skinless fillet and brush it with egg white. Transfer the seasoned flour to a long, shallow bowl or dish. Dip both sides of each fillet into the flour mixture. Brush off any excess flour before placing the fillets in the pan.

Making Guacamole and Serving

- In a bowl, mash the avocado using a fork.

- Add the other guacamole ingredients, and, using the fork, mix well.

- Assemble your tacos by scooping the fish into a tortilla, then sprinkling in some of the lettuce.

- Finally, scoop some of the guacamole over the top and finish with a sprig of cilantro.

SPRING PASTA

A colorful springtime pasta makes for a satisfying and healthy lunch

This simple and fresh pasta dish incorporates ripe cherry tomatoes, tender asparagus tips, and fresh mozzarella. But the key to the pasta is the peppery fresh basil, which is said to have anti-inflammatory effects and antibacterial properties. Asparagus boasts its own health benefits, as it's believed to be a natural diuretic. And tomatoes, like many brightly colored fruits, are packed with antioxidants.

The vegetarian version of this pasta is fresh and light, invoking the season for which it is named. But adding a bit of Prosciutto di Parma to the pasta makes it heartier with an extra dose of protein.

Yield: 1

Ingredients

¹/₂ cup asparagus tips

2 ounces dry penne pasta

2 tablespoons olive oil

2 cloves garlic, minced

¹/₂ cup cherry tomatoes, halved

¹/₄ cup chopped fresh basil leaves

3 ounces fresh buffalo mozzarella, cubed (or use mini bocconcini)

1 tablespoon grated Parmesan cheese

Sea salt and freshly ground pepper, to taste

Calories 700, **Fat** (g) 44, **Carbohydrates** (g) 50, **Protein** (g) 26, **Fiber** (g) 5, **Saturated Fat** (g) 15, **Cholesterol** (mg) 60, **Sodium** (mg) 714

Spring Pasta

- In a medium-size pot, bring 1 cup of water to a boil.

- Place asparagus in a steamer in the pot and cover.

- Cook 5–7 minutes, depending on the thickness of the tips and the desired texture.

- In a large pot, bring a quart of salted water to boil. Add pasta; cook 12–15 minutes or until al dente, then drain.

- Sauté garlic, tomatoes, and basil. Add pasta and asparagus to mixture, top with cheeses and salt and pepper, and serve.

Smoky Spring Pasta: Instead of using fresh mozzarella, try a smoked mozzarella to increase the depth of flavor of this dish. Prepare the dish as described below, but use 3 ounces of smoked mozzarella, either cubed or in bocconcini (mini balls) format.

Spring Pasta with Prosciutto: When it comes to Prosciutto di Parma, a little goes a long way. Take 1 ounce of prosciutto and chop it into thin slivers. Add it to the tomato, garlic, and basil sauté to add an extra savory dimension to the pasta.

Mincing Garlic

Sautéing Veggies

- Cut off the ends of your cloves of garlic. With the skins still on the cloves, use the heel of your palm against the flat edge of a sharp chef's knife to smash them. The skins should slip right off.

- First, slice the garlic into thin slivers. Then, rock the chef's knife back and forth over the slices until the garlic is all in tiny pieces.

- Use the edge of the knife to gather the minced garlic into a small mound, and rock the chef's knife back and forth over the mound until no big chunks of garlic remain.

- In a saucepan over medium heat, add half the oil.

- Add the garlic, and sauté for 30 seconds, then add the tomatoes and basil leaves.

- Sauté for another minute or so, then remove from heat. Add the cooked pasta, steamed asparagus, buffalo mozzarella, and the rest of the olive oil.

- Toss with the Parmesan and salt and pepper, and serve.

THREE-BEAN SALAD

This easy salad is packed with fiber and bunches of other important nutrients

Beans are good for your heart, or so the old rhyme goes. But beans have more health benefits than just that. They are an excellent source of soluble fiber, which can help lower cholesterol. In particular, black beans, cannellini beans, and chickpeas (garbanzo beans) each contain a trace mineral that can help detoxify sulfites. Most beans have twice the iron that

beef has, and beans are also rich in magnesium, deficiencies of which have been associated with heart attacks.

We've suggested using chickpeas, black beans and cannellini beans, but feel free to add whatever beans you like. We tend to think a salad is best put together by color, so feel free to add green or red beans to brighten yours. *Yield: 4 servings*

Ingredients

1 cup canned chickpeas, drained

1 cup canned black beans, drained

1 cup canned cannellini beans, drained

$1/2$ red onion, diced small

$1/4$ cup finely chopped fresh parsley

$1/2$ cup vinaigrette (recipe follows)

Sea salt and freshly ground pepper, to taste

For the vinaigrette:

$1/2$ cup olive oil

$1/4$ cup red wine vinegar

$1/4$ cup fresh lemon juice

2 teaspoons Dijon mustard

2 cloves garlic

Calories 297, **Fat** (g) 15, **Carbohydrates** (g) 31, **Protein** (g) 11, **Fiber** (g) 9, **Saturated Fat** (g) 2, **Cholesterol** (mg) 0, **Sodium** (mg) 484

Three-bean Salad

- For the vinaigrette: Combine all the ingredients in a blender and blend until smooth.

- For the salad: Rinse all the beans under cold water and drain.

- In a salad bowl, combine the beans, onion, and parsley.

- Toss the contents of the bowl with the vinaigrette and salt and pepper, and serve.

Add kidney beans to your salad. Like other beans, they not only contain slow-burning carbs but also offer an extra dose of iron for energy. They also add a splash of bright color, and a substantial meaty texture to the dish.

Four Bean Salad: To add a different splash of color to your salad—not to mention a fresh crunch--chop up and steam 1 cup green beans until they are al dente. Toss them into your salad with the other ingredients.

Chopping Parsley

Soaking Your Own Beans

- Parsley is also good for your heart. It contains folic acid, which, among other things, is important for vascular health.

- Clean the parsley by soaking it in a cold water bath for a few minutes. Repeat once or twice.

- Remove the leaves from the stems, then gather them into a mound.

- Take a sharp chef's knife and finely slice the parsley. Using the edge of the knife, gather it back into a mound, and rock the knife back and forth until the parsley is finely chopped.

- Instead of using canned beans, you can soak your own. Place dry beans in a bowl and pick out any small stones, as well as any discolored beans.

- Pour three times as much water as beans over the beans, cover, and let sit overnight.

- Soak different kinds of beans separately, as they each take different amounts of time to moisten.

- Drain the beans and pour them into a pot of boiling water. Cook them until tender.

QUICK LUNCH

TURKEY BLT

Bacon, lettuce, and tomato can be light when the "B" is of the turkey variety

You know what the letters in this diner mainstay stand for. But a BLT doesn't have to be loaded with fat and calories. You can reduce both in this lunchtime standard by replacing traditional bacon with turkey bacon, which generally has about half the fat of pork bacon. Look for all-natural turkey bacon that is free of nitrates.

You can also try making this sandwich with a low-sodium bacon. The portion size should be smaller than if you use turkey bacon, however.

Beef up your BLT with a couple slices of roasted turkey or chicken, or spice it up with a little extra heat.

Yield: 1 sandwich

Ingredients

2 slices whole wheat bread

3 strips turkey bacon

1–2 leaves romaine lettuce

½ tomato, sliced

1 tablespoon light mayonnaise (optional)

Sea salt and freshly ground pepper, to taste

Turkey BLT

- Toast the bread in a toaster or toaster oven.

- In a pan over medium-high heat, cook the bacon for a few minutes on each side until browned.

- Place the cooked bacon on a paper towel to soak up the excess grease.

- Assemble sandwich with lettuce, tomato, mayo, and salt and pepper.

Calories 305, **Fat** (g) 12, **Carbohydrates** (g) 30, **Protein** (g) 24, **Fiber** (g) 5, **Saturated Fat** (g) 1, **Cholesterol** (mg) 75, **Sodium** (mg) 1006

Roasted Turkey BLT: Beef up your sandwich with two ¼-inch slices of roasted turkey or chicken. You can buy sliced turkey or chicken from the deli counter at the supermarket, or use leftover chicken or turkey that you prepared at home.

Turkey BLT with Chipotle Mayo: Give your BLT an extra kick with a quick and easy chipotle mayonnaise. Stir 1 tablespoon of canned chipotle chiles in adobo sauce into ¼ cup of low-fat mayo. Spread 1 tablespoon of the mayo onto your sandwich as you assemble.

Slicing Tomatoes

- Using a paring knife, remove the stem and core of the tomato.

- With a sharp serrated knife, halve your tomato.

- Slice half of the tomato into ¼-inch slices.

Assembling the BLT

- Assemble your BLT by layering the bacon, tomato, and lettuce on the bread.

- Spread the mayo (or substitute mustard) on the top slice, close the sandwich, and serve.

QUICK LUNCH

TORTILLA SOUP

A satisfying crunch can be found at the bottom of this soup bowl

Tortilla soup is a hearty yet simple Mexican dish that was born out of leftovers. Making use of leftover cooked chicken and stale tortillas, it became a staple of the cuisine.

Our version makes use of the kinds of fresh and canned ingredients people tend to have lying around the house. Make your soup, then pour it over the stale tortilla chips so that they retain their crunch. By using baked tortilla chips, you'll be cutting calories and more than half the fat found in regular tortilla chips. We've suggested a vegetarian version of the soup, but because it contains tofu, you won't miss out on any of the protein in the original version.

Yield: 2

Ingredients

2 cups chicken stock

2 cloves garlic

¹/₂ cup chopped canned tomatoes with juice

¹/₂ cup canned black beans, drained and rinsed

¹/₂ cup canned corn kernels, drained and rinsed

1 teaspoon cumin

¹/₄ cup finely chopped fresh cilantro

1 cup leftover cubed cooked chicken

Juice of ¹/₂ lime

¹/₂ cup slightly crushed baked tortilla chips

1 dollop low-fat sour cream

Calories 356, **Fat** (g) 9, **Carbohydrates** (g) 38, **Protein** (g) 31, **Fiber** (g) 7, **Saturated Fat** (g) 3, **Cholesterol** (mg) 62, **Sodium** (mg) 1010

Tortilla Soup

- Pour the chicken stock into a large pot.

- Over medium-high heat, bring the chicken stock to a boil. Reduce the heat, and let the stock simmer. Roast garlic, then mince.

- Add the tomatoes, beans, corn, garlic, and cumin to the pot. Simmer 10–15 minutes, then add cilantro, lime juice and chicken.

- Simmer another 5–10 minutes, then remove from heat. Prepare a bowl with chips; add soup and sour cream.

Vegetarian Tortilla Soup: Instead of canned beans, feel free to use dried beans, soaking and cooking them yourself. You can also replace the canned corn with fresh corn right off the cob. To make this soup into a vegetarian dish, simply replace the cubed chicken pieces with 1 cup cubed tofu and replace the chicken stock with 2 cups vegetable stock. Try using smoked tofu for a deep, smoky flavor.

Smoky Tortilla Soup: To add a smoky dimension to your soup, prepare it as described below, but use 1 cup cubed smoked chicken instead of leftover cooked chicken. You can find smoked chicken at the deli counter at the supermarket.

Roasting Garlic

- To roast the garlic, heat a dry pan over high heat.

- Roast the garlic for several minutes on each side, until the skins are browned and the flesh is softened.

- Remove from heat, then smash with the flat side of a chef's knife. Mince garlic.

Pouring Soup over Chips

- Dump the crushed tortilla chips into a soup bowl.

- Pour a cup of the soup over the chips and finish with a dollop of sour cream.

QUICK LUNCH

CHICKEN LETTUCE WRAPS

This Asian-inspired lunch will please everyone at the table

This Asian-inspired dish can be whipped up easily if you happen to have leftover chicken and a head of lettuce in the fridge.

Like tacos and fajitas, lettuce wraps are a fun, do-it-yourself idea for dinner. Simply put out all the elements—the chicken, the lettuce, the sauces—and let your dinner companions put together their own wraps. Don't worry about things getting messy: It's all part of the fun!

A trip to an Asian market for Vietnamese pickled carrots or Japanese pickled daikon will make your wraps extra special, as will a squirt of spicy Asian Sriracha sauce.
Yield: 1 serving (4 wraps)

Ingredients

1 tablespoon vegetable oil

¹/₂ cup chopped mushrooms

¹/₂ pound cooked chicken, cubed or shredded

¹/₂ cup chopped canned water chestnuts

¹/₄ cup chopped scallions

¹/₄ cup diced bell pepper

1 tablespoon grated fresh ginger

2 tablespoons soy sauce

2 tablespoons hoisin sauce

1 tablespoon grated fresh orange zest

4–6 large butter lettuce leaves

Calories 522.6, **Fat** (g) 20.1, **Carbohydrates** (g) 36.5, **Protein** (g) 48.2, **Fiber** (g) 4.1, **Saturated Fat** (g) 2.7, **Cholesterol** (mg) 120, **Sodium** (mg) 2689.3

Chicken Lettuce Wraps

- In a sauté pan or wok over medium heat, heat up the oil and add the mushrooms.

- Cook until soft, then add the chicken, water chestnuts, scallions, bell pepper, ginger, and soy sauce.

- Sauté for a few more minutes before tossing in the hoisin sauce and orange zest.

- Stir the contents of the pan until everything is coated with the hoisin, then remove from heat. Assemble wraps in lettuce leaves and serve.

Crunchy Chicken Lettuce Wraps: Make the recipe as directed below, except toss ½ cup julienned carrots into your chicken mixture for extra color and crunch. If you can find pickled carrots or daikon, these will add a savory dimension to the wrap.

Spicy Chicken Lettuce Wraps: For extra kick, dose your wrap with a squirt of Sriracha sauce, the popular Asian hot pepper and garlic condiment. Sriracha is becoming more popular across the U.S. and can be found in most regular supermarkets, as well as in Asian markets.

Chopping Ingredients

- The lettuce leaves are delicate, so it's important to chop the ingredients finely.

- If you're shredding your chicken, use a skinless poached or roasted chicken breast or thigh.

- Lay your chicken on a work surface and, using a fork, break up the chicken by running the fork along the fibers of the meat.

Spooning Chicken into Lettuce

- Assemble your wraps by spooning the chicken mixture onto each of the lettuce leaves.

- Be careful with the delicate lettuce.

- Fold over the lettuce leaves to loosely close each wrap, and serve.

QUICK LUNCH

SPINACH STRAWBERRY SALAD

Adding fruit to green salads gives them a touch of sweetness and color

Some people still feel funny about adding fruit to their green salads. But you shouldn't, especially when you consider that tomatoes and cucumbers, which are regularly added to salads, are fruit. This summery salad incorporates tender baby spinach, creamy avocado, and sweet strawberries for a tasty and nutrient-rich dish.

You may have heard that avocados are high in fat. That's true, but it's important to note that avocados contain mono-unsaturated fat, a good fat that actually helps lower cholesterol. Avocados are also an excellent source of potassium, which helps regulate blood pressure.

You may enjoy it without the dressing, if you like. *Yield: 1*

Ingredients

3 ounces fresh baby spinach

1 cup sliced strawberries

1/2 avocado, sliced

1 ounce crumbled semisoft goat cheese

3 tablespoons vinaigrette (recipe follows)

For the vinaigrette:

1/2 cup olive oil

1/4 cup raspberry vinegar

2 tablespoons honey

2 teaspoons Dijon mustard

2 cloves garlic

Calories 587, **Fat** (g) 45, **Carbohydrates** (g) 42, **Protein** (g) 12, **Fiber** (g) 12, **Saturated Fat** (g) 11, **Cholesterol** (mg) 22, **Sodium** (mg) 313

Spinach Strawberry Salad

- For the vinaigrette: Combine all the ingredients in a blender and blend until smooth.

- For the salad: Combine all the ingredients in a salad bowl and toss with the vinaigrette until evenly coated.

Opening an Avocado

- To open an avocado, use a sharp chef's knife. Slice the avocado in half lengthwise, cutting around the pit.

- Separate the two halves and take the side containing the pit.

- With your knife, carefully but firmly strike the pit of the avocado, hard enough for the knife to become stuck in the pit.

- Hold the avocado half, and simply turn the pit using the knife as a handle. It should pop right out. Peel each half.

Crumbling Goat Cheese

- To crumble the goat cheese, simply break it up using your fingers.

- Depending on the texture of your goat cheese, it might not crumble easily. In this case, cube it.

QUICK LUNCH

CHICKEN ARUGULA SALAD
Peppery green arugula makes this salad a hearty affair

Arugula, also known as rocket, is a leafy green that is an excellent source of antioxidants. A nutrient-rich base for a salad, it contains vitamins A and C, folic acid, and calcium, which are, respectively, crucial to eye, immune system, heart, and bone health.

This hearty salad also contains fiber-rich cannellini beans and antioxidant-packed tomatoes. The dressing also incorporates garlic, which has been shown to be a natural antibiotic, among a slew of other health benefits.

Yield: 1

Ingredients

2 tablespoons balsamic vinegar

2 teaspoons grainy mustard

4 tablespoons olive oil, divided

1 clove garlic, minced

1/4 pound leftover cooked chicken, cut into bite-size pieces

Sea salt and freshly ground black pepper, to taste

3 cups arugula leaves, rinsed and patted dry

1/2 cup cherry tomatoes, halved

1/2 cup canned cannellini beans, drained and rinsed

1 ounce grated Parmesan cheese

Calories 702, **Fat** (g) 46, **Carbohydrates** (g) 28, **Protein** (g) 43, **Fiber** (g) 8, **Saturated Fat** (g) 11, **Cholesterol** (mg) 84, **Sodium** (mg) 1157

Chicken Arugula Salad

- For the vinaigrette: Combine the vinegar, mustard, and 3 tablespoons olive oil in a small bowl and whisk.

- In a sauté pan over medium heat, heat up the remaining 1 tablespoon oil, then toss in the garlic, chicken, and salt and pepper.

- Sauté for a few minutes until the chicken is warmed through before removing from heat.

- In a salad bowl, combine the arugula, tomatoes, and beans. Add the chicken, and toss with the vinaigrette.

- Top with Parmesan cheese.

We recommend heating up the chicken in a pan, but this step can be skipped. If you're in a rush, just use cold cooked chicken. If you have more time, you can use fresh chicken and cook it specifically for this dish.

Ham & Arugula Salad: Make the recipe as directed below, except instead of using cooked chicken, try tossing in ¼ pound cubed cooked ham. You can sauté your ham if you like, or just toss it into the salad cold.

Whisking Vinaigrette

- Whisk the olive oil together with the vinegar and mustard until all the ingredients are well incorporated.

Sautéing Chicken

- The chicken is already cooked, so you need not sauté it for too long. You're simply sautéing to lightly brown it and warm it up.

- If you prefer to use fresh chicken, sauté it for longer—up to 15 minutes over medium-high heat—to make sure it has cooked through.

BUTTERNUT SQUASH SOUP

A puree of sweet squash is the base for this satisfying soup

Winter squash is a terrific ingredient to stock up on, not only for its array of health benefits, but also because of its long shelf life. Of course, the health benefits are nothing to sniff at. Loaded with beta-carotene, vitamin C, potassium, and fiber, butternut squash can help promote heart, immune system, and digestive health.

This soup is full of flavor and fortified with extra nutrients from the added ginger. Aromatic, zingy ginger has been found to promote digestive health and improve circulation.

Enjoy this pretty bowl of bright orange sunshine with a piece of crusty whole wheat bread for a satisfying meal on a cool or rainy day.

Yield: 6 servings

Ingredients

1 tablespoon olive oil

1/2 yellow onion, diced small

1 quart chicken stock

1 butternut squash, peeled and cubed

2 tablespoons grated fresh ginger

1 teaspoon nutmeg

Sea salt and freshly ground black pepper, to taste

Calories 70, **Fat** (g) 2.5, **Carbohydrates** (g) 10.3, **Protein** (g) 3, **Fiber** (g) 1.6, **Saturated Fat** (g) 0.4, **Cholesterol** (mg) 0, **Sodium** (mg) 476.4

Butternut Squash Soup

- In a large pot over medium-high heat, heat up the oil and add the onion.

- Cook the onion until soft, then pour three-quarters of the stock over it. Increase the heat to bring it to a boil.

- Add the squash, ginger, nutmeg, and salt and pepper. Simmer 30 minutes. Then transfer to a blender and blend. Return soup to the pot; stir in remaining stock as needed. Serve.

• • • • RECIPE VARIATION • • • •

Roasted Butternut Squash Soup: Try making this soup with roasted squash for a greater depth of flavor. Peel and cube the squash, and toss it with olive oil, a pinch of salt, 1 or 2 tablespoons of brown sugar, and a pinch of cinnamon. Place the squash in a baking dish. In an oven preheated to 400°F, bake the squash for 45 minutes to 1 hour, or until tender. Be sure to turn the squash at least once during the baking period. Remove the squash from the oven and toss it in the blender with the other ingredients.

Simmering the Soup

- After you add the squash, reduce the heat and allow the soup to simmer for 30 minutes or so, until the squash is soft.

- Later, when you return the blended mixture to the pot, you may want to add more stock to reach your desired consistency.

Blending Ingredients

- Once the squash has softened, dump the contents of the pot into a blender and blend until smooth.

- Be careful when handling the hot contents of the pot. Be sure to seal the blender before turning it on.

TURKISH RED LENTIL SOUP

Boost your energy and fill your belly with a hearty red lentil soup

Lentils come in all sorts of colors, from green to red to yellow to black. Slightly lighter in texture and flavor, red lentils boast almost all the same health benefits as their green counterparts. This soup is made with the red kind, but any type of lentil will work. A great source of dietary fiber, lentils are also high in iron, and so can really help boost your energy level. We recommend making this version with a pinch of paprika, but you can toss in more than a pinch if you like. Paprika is unusually high in vitamin C and can help regulate blood pressure, improve circulation, and facilitate digestion. *Yield: 6*

Ingredients

4 cups beef stock

1 cup red lentils, rinsed and drained

1/4 cup uncooked rice

1 large onion, quartered

1 large carrot, peeled and roughly chopped

2 tablespoons tomato paste

2 tablespoons olive oil

Pinch of paprika flakes

Salt and freshly ground pepper, to taste

Calories 210, **Fat** (g) 6, **Carbohydrates** (g) 30, **Protein** (g) 11, **Fiber** (g) 5, **Saturated Fat** (g) 1, **Cholesterol** (mg) 0, **Sodium** (mg) 538

Turkish Red Lentil Soup

- In a large saucepan over high heat, bring the stock to a boil.

- Add the lentils, rice, onion, and carrot, and simmer for about 30 minutes, or until the lentils are cooked.

- Stir occasionally to ensure the lentils don't stick to the bottom of the pan. Skim off any scum on the surface.

- In a blender, blend the soup until smooth. Return soup to saucepan and, over low heat, stir in the tomato paste, olive oil, paprika, salt and pepper. Serve.

• • • • RECIPE VARIATION • • • •

Stockless Turkish Red Lentil Soup: Prepare the soup as described below but instead of beef stock, you can use chicken stock or even just plain water. The latter won't have as much flavor as stock, but it will do in a pinch.

Spicy Turkish Red Lentil Soup: Changing up the spices used will slightly alter the flavor profile of the soup—not to mention its nutritional value. Try adding a pinch of cumin, which is great for digestive health, or 2–3 cloves of immune-boosting garlic, finely minced.

Chopping Carrots

- To peel the carrots, use a potato peeler. With the blade side down, slide the peeler along the length of the carrot, as though shaving it.

- Rotate the carrot and repeat until the entire surface is peeled.

- To chop roughly, use a sharp chef's knife. Chop the carrot into chunks about 2 inches long.

Skimming Surface of Soup

- As the soup simmers, proteins rise to the surface and create a foamlike substance on the soup.

- To get rid of it, use a spoon or skimmer. Run the skimmer along the surface of the soup, about ¼-inch deep.

- Scoop up the scum, then discard it.

TURKEY CHILI
Sometimes a hot bowl of chili is just what the doctor ordered

It's the food of cook-offs and Super Bowl parties. But chili can also be a nutritious lunchtime meal. We make this version with lean ground turkey meat, but you can swap out the turkey for beef. As you know, turkey meat isn't always the least fatty option. Be sure to specify lean ground turkey meat at your butcher's. If you do opt for beef, look for ground sirloin, which is one of the leanest cuts of beef. Ground chuck will be fattier.

In either case, opt for free-range, antibiotic-free meat to ensure that you aren't consuming extra preservatives or hormones.

Packed with beans and hot peppers, this chili is not only satisfying for the belly, but healthy for the heart.

Yield: 6 servings

Ingredients

1–2 tablespoons olive oil

1 large yellow onion, diced small

4 cloves garlic, minced

1 pound lean free-range antibiotic-free ground turkey

1 tablespoon ground cumin

Sea salt and freshly ground pepper, to taste

1/4 cup light Mexican beer (optional to deglaze pan)

2 cups canned crushed tomatoes

1 cup black beans

1 jalapeño or habañero chile, seeded and chopped

2 tablespoons chili powder

1/2 cup finely chopped fresh cilantro

Dollop of low-fat sour cream

Calories 220, **Fat** (g) 10, **Carbohydrates** (g) 16, **Protein** (g) 17, **Fiber** (g) 4, **Saturated Fat** (g) 3, **Cholesterol** (mg) 60, **Sodium** (mg) 526

Turkey Chili

- Heat oil in a saucepan over medium heat, then add the onion. Cook until soft. Add garlic, and cook a few more minutes.

- Remove onions from the saucepan; add turkey, cumin, and salt and pepper.

- Cook turkey 5–10 minutes, then remove from pan and deglaze. Toss onions and garlic back into the saucepan and mix into turkey. Add tomatoes, black beans, chiles, and chili powder.

- Simmer chili 10 minutes, then add cilantro. Season and add a dollop of sour cream on each serving.

• • • • RECIPE VARIATION • • • •

Vegetarian Chili: You can turn this recipe into vegetarian chili in a few easy steps. First, of course, omit the turkey. Second, add more beans. In addition to the black beans, dump 1 cup of kidney beans and 1 cup of white beans into the chili. Add ½ cup of fresh or canned corn kernels, as well as a diced bell pepper and a chopped carrot. Use the same seasonings—especially the healthy dose of cumin and fresh chiles—and you won't even miss the meat.

Cooking Turkey

- When cooking the turkey, you might need to add a bit more oil.

- Stir intermittently so that it cooks evenly.

- You should deglaze the pan before adding ingredients back into it.

- To deglaze the saucepan, pour in the beer and scrape up the browned bits, then allow most of the liquid to cook off.

Stirring Chili

- The chili should simmer for 10 minutes or so before you stir in the cilantro.

- Remember to stir intermittently so that the chili cooks evenly.

TUNA MELT

This toasty, cheesy sandwich is as easy to make as opening a can

This satisfying sandwich incorporates wallet-friendly canned tuna, crunchy celery, and melted cheddar. We recommend reading your tuna can label before buying to ensure you're getting good fish that has been harvested in an earth-friendly way. Look for albacore tuna from the United States' Pacific coast.

Tuna is not only an excellent source of protein, but it is also high in omega-3 fatty acids, which are known to promote cardiovascular health. In order to maintain healthy omega-3 levels in the body, it is recommended to eat two servings of tuna or salmon per week. Our bodies don't actually make their own omega-3s so we have to get them by consuming them in foods.

Yield: 2 servings

Ingredients

1 can albacore tuna packed in water

2 tablespoons low-fat mayonnaise

2 tablespoons chopped fresh dill

1 tablespoon lemon juice

1 teaspoon Dijon mustard

1 stalk celery, finely chopped

1 ounce grated cheddar cheese

4 slices whole wheat bread

Calories 368, **Fat** (g) 15, **Carbohydrates** (g) 30, **Protein** (g) 30, **Fiber** (g) 5, **Saturated Fat** (g) 5, **Cholesterol** (mg) 51, **Sodium** (mg) 866

Tuna Melt

- In a mixing bowl, combine the tuna, mayonnaise, dill, lemon juice, mustard, and celery.

- Mix ingredients well, breaking up the tuna with a fork so that it is well coated with dressing.

- Sprinkle the cheese on half the bread slices. Toast all the bread until the cheese is melted.

- Assemble sandwiches and serve.

···· RECIPE VARIATION ····

Spicy Tuna Melt: Spice up your tuna melt by trying this recipe with 1 ounce of a spicy Pepper Jack cheese instead of cheddar. Grate the cheese onto one slice of bread and toast it, along with a second slice of bread with no cheese, in a toaster oven for 10 minutes. Assemble with tuna mixture, as described below.

Toasting Bread and Cheese

- To toast your bread, use a toaster oven or a conventional oven heated to 350°F.

- Toast the bread for about 10 minutes, or until it's lightly browned and the cheese starts to bubble.

Assembling Tuna Melt

- Assemble your melt by scooping the tuna mixture onto the toasted bread.

- Close the sandwich with the cheese-covered slice.

- Press lightly to hold sandwich together.

121

PANINI MARGHERITA

This pressed Italian sandwich is as simple as it is satisfying

This pressed sandwich is like the Italian version of a grilled cheese sandwich. A panini (actually a panino; *panini* is the plural term) is just a sandwich in Italy. But we've come to know *panini* to mean an Italian-style pressed sandwich. This simple panini is made of fresh vine-ripened tomatoes, creamy buffalo mozzarella cheese, and peppery leaves of basil. It is named for Queen Margherita of Italy, and features the colors of the Italian flag.

You can add almost anything that you would normally add to a sandwich to your panini. Layer cured meats or even tuna salad with cheese for a warm, satisfying lunchtime meal.
Yield: 1 sandwich

Ingredients

1 whole wheat baguette or sub roll

2 vine-ripened tomatoes, sliced

2 ounces buffalo mozzarella, sliced

5 leaves of fresh basil

Sea salt and freshly ground pepper, to taste

Panini Margherita

- Slice the baguette or roll in half lengthwise.

- Layer the tomatoes, mozzarella, and basil leaves on one of the slices of bread.

- Sprinkle salt and pepper over the top before closing the sandwich.

- Press sandwich and serve.

Calories 374, **Fat** (g) 18, **Carbohydrates** (g) 31, **Protein** (g) 22, **Fiber** (g) 6, **Saturated Fat** (g) 11, **Cholesterol** (mg) 60, **Sodium** (mg) 1007

····· RECIPE VARIATIONS ·····

Panini Fontina: Try this sandwich with a different cheese to completely change its flavor profile. How about an aged fontina, for a more intense and saltier taste? Fontina can range from a harder aged cheese to a milder, creamier young version.

Olive Panini Margherita: Add a new layer to the flavors by spreading olive tapenade on one half of the sandwich. Take 1½ tablespoons of olive tapenade and spread onto one half of the cold sandwich. Assemble and press it as described below.

Pressing the Sandwich

- Take the cold sandwich and place it in a preheated sandwich press. Close the lid.

- Press the sandwich until the bread is toasted and the cheese begins to melt.

- Remove from the press and serve immediately.

Sandwich Press Substitute

- If you don't have a sandwich press, spray a skillet with olive oil. Place the sandwich in the skillet over medium-high heat.

- You may also want to lightly spray the sandwich with olive oil.

- Cover the bottom of a smaller skillet or a small pot with tinfoil. Use it to press down on the panini in the pan.

- Flip the panini and repeat this process until the bread is well toasted and the mozzarella begins to melt a little.

CHICKEN & RICE SOUP

Warm your soul and feed your body with this simple savory soup

Chicken soup is good not only for the soul, but also for the body. Medical research has shown that the combination of chicken and vegetables in hot liquid can help fight colds and soothe other respiratory infections.

This recipe calls for chicken stock, which you can buy or easily make yourself by boiling a chicken carcass in a pot of water with carrots, onions, celery, herbs, salt, and pepper. Let it simmer for 4–5 hours, then strain.

This recipe calls for brown rice, which has more than three times as much fiber as white rice has. Brown rice is also a source of magnesium, manganese and zinc.

Yield: 1

Ingredients

1 tablespoon olive oil

l yellow onion, diced

1 carrot, chopped

1 stalk celery, chopped

Sea salt and freshly ground pepper, to taste

1 cup leftover chicken, cubed or shredded

3 cups chicken stock

¼ cup chopped fresh thyme

1 bay leaf

⅓ cup uncooked brown rice

Calories 752, **Fat** (g) 26, **Carbohydrates** (g) 69, **Protein** (g) 58, **Fiber** (g) 6, **Saturated Fat** (g) 5, **Cholesterol** (mg) 118, **Sodium** (mg) 2308

Chicken & Rice Soup

- In a saucepan over medium-high heat, heat up the oil and add the onion.

- Sauté the onion for a few minutes before adding the carrot, celery, and salt and pepper.

- Throw in the chicken and sauté for a minute or two.

- Add the stock, thyme, and bay leaf. Simmer 15–20 minutes. Add the rice and simmer until cooked. Serve.

• • • • • RECIPE VARIATIONS • • • • •

Chicken and Vegetable Soup: You can add any number of vegetables to this soup, from parsnips to turnips to fennel. Instead of rice, throw two raw quartered peeled baby potatoes into the pot, and let them cook for 15–20 minutes in the broth with the other vegetables.

Chicken Noodle Soup: What better way is there to enjoy a hot bowl of chicken soup than with noodles? Instead of rice, take ½ ounce dried linguine or other pasta noodles, break them in half, and add them to the simmering pot of broth and vegetables.

Soup Simmering

- Add the stock, thyme, and bay leaf and bring the soup to a temperature just shy of boiling.

- Reduce the heat to a simmer. Allow the soup to simmer for 15–20 minutes or longer before adding the rice.

Adding Rice

- After adding the rice, let the soup simmer for another 20 minutes or so, until the rice is cooked. Then serve.

HUMMUS & CARROT STICKS
This fiber-rich Mediterranean dip is sure to tide you over

Hummus is a tasty, easy snack you can make at home. Chick-peas (a.k.a. garbanzo beans) make for a virtually fat-free pro-tein and are high in fiber, which can help lower cholesterol, as well as prevent digestive disorders. And tahini, a sesame seed paste that originated in the Mediterranean, is a great source of calcium, protein, and vitamin B.

You can use canned chickpeas for this recipe or soak your own dried beans. One serving of hummus is just 2–3 tablespoons, so use it as a dip for carrots or other veggies.

You can also use hummus as a spread on sandwiches and wraps.

Yield: 2 servings

Ingredients

³/₄ cup canned chickpeas

Juice of 1 lemon

2 tablespoons fresh orange juice

1 clove garlic

1¹/₂ tablespoons tahini

Pinch of sea salt

1 cup baby carrots

Calories 169, **Fat** (g) 7, **Carbohydrates** (g) 22, **Protein** (g) 7,
Fiber (g) 6, **Saturated Fat** (g) 1, **Cholesterol** (mg) 0,
Sodium (mg) 374

Hummus and Carrot Sticks

- If using canned chickpeas, rinse them under cold water.

- If using dried chickpeas, soak 1 cup of them in a pot for 6–8 hours. Drain and rinse the soaked beans, then return them to the pot and add 2 cups of cold water. Bring to a boil for 10 minutes. Skim foam off top; then simmer for 1 hour or until chickpeas are fork-tender. Use ¾ of these for the hummus.

- In a blender, combine all the ingredients except carrots and blend until smooth. Serve with carrots or with other veggies.

• • • • RECIPE VARIATIONS • • • •

Hummus with Toasted Pine Nuts: Place a tablespoon of pine nuts on a cookie sheet and spray lightly with olive oil. In an oven preheated to 250 degrees, toast them for 5–10 minutes. Remove pine nuts from heat and sprinkle on top of your finished hummus.

Hummus & Cut Veggies: Instead of carrots, serve your hummus with celery sticks, radishes and sliced bell peppers. Cut celery stalks into 3-inch sticks, cut ends off radishes and halve, and seed and slice yellow and red bell peppers into strips for dipping.

Juicing Lemons

- There are several popular methods for juicing lemons.

- First, slice your lemon in half. Take one half and, using a glass or plastic juicer, firmly twist the lemon over the core of the juicer.

- Alternatively, simply take a fork to each lemon half. Working over a bowl, twist the fork to break up the segments as you squeeze the juice out of the lemon.

Blending Ingredients

- To adjust the consistency of the hummus, add water by the tablespoon while it's still in the blender, and blend again.

- Be careful not to overblend. Use the high setting for short spurts at a time to be sure.

TABOULI

Parsley takes center stage in this signature Mediterranean dish

The main ingredient in this fresh and light Mediterranean snack is bulgur, a cereal similar to cracked wheat.

Bulgur contains more nutrients than rice or couscous—specifically, it has twice the fiber of brown rice, not to mention fewer calories and less fat.

The other main ingredient in tabouli is parsley. We recommend using Italian parsley, if possible. More than just a decorative garnish, this hearty herb is rich in antioxidants, as well as vitamins A and C. You can also make this recipe with quinoa instead of bulgur. Although quinoa looks and acts like a grain, it is not. In fact, it provides an unusually complete protein.

Yield: 4

Ingredients

³/₄ cup cooked cracked wheat bulgur

2 tablespoons olive oil

Juice of ¹/₂ lemon

¹/₂ scallion, chopped (green part only)

¹/₂ cup finely chopped fresh parsley

2 tablespoons finely chopped fresh mint

1 tomato, chopped

¹/₂ cucumber, chopped

Pinch of paprika

Pinch of cayenne pepper

Sea salt, to taste

Tabouli

- In a mixing bowl, combine the rest of the ingredients with the cooked bulgur.

- Once the bulgur and other ingredients are well incorporated, chill the tabouli, then serve over lettuce or with pita bread.

Calories 160, **Fat** (g) 7, **Carbohydrates** (g) 22, **Protein** (g) 4, **Fiber** (g) 5, **Saturated Fat** (g) 1, **Cholesterol** (mg) 0, **Sodium** (mg) 85

Quinoa Tabouli: For a twist on this dish, use quinoa instead of bulgur. Bring ¾ cup of quinoa and enough water to cover it to a boil, then let it stand for 10 minutes, or until all the water is absorbed. Rinse and drain the quinoa before adding it to the tabouli.

Millet Tabouli: Prepare the recipe as is described below, except use millet instead of bulgur. Add 1 part millet to 1½ parts boiling water. Reduce heat to a simmer for 20–25 minutes or until all the water is absorbed. Then, let stand for 5 minutes before mixing with other ingredients.

Cooking Bulgur

- To make the bulgur, bring 1½ cups water to a boil in a small pot over high heat.

- Pour in the bulgur and turn off the heat. Let the bulgur stand until all the water is absorbed, 30 minutes to an hour.

- Drain any excess liquid.

Combining Ingredients

- Make sure the ingredients are mixed well before chilling. Serve tabouli cold.

KALE CHIPS

These crispy "chips" pack antioxidants, calcium, fiber—and flavor

Kale is one of the foods recently dubbed a superfood. It's an excellent source of vitamin A and beta-carotene, which when combined promote ocular health. Kale's other antioxidants help to detoxify the body's cells and reduce the risk of various cancers.

For this recipe, you can use green kale or red kale or even a combination of the two for a colorful final result. We've suggested seasoning the chips with a little sea salt, and maybe a pinch of cayenne pepper. But you can really add whatever flavors you like to them. A little garlic powder or paprika will add new flavor dimensions to the snack.
Yield: 1

Ingredients

2 tablespoons olive oil

$^1/_2$ tablespoon apple cider vinegar

2 cups chopped kale (bite-size pieces)

Sea salt, to taste

Kale Chips

- In a mixing bowl, combine the olive oil and vinegar and whisk well.

- Toss this with the kale until all the leaves are well coated. Line a baking sheet with parchment paper.

- Spread out the kale on the sheet and sprinkle it with salt.

- In an oven preheated to 400°F, bake the kale for 15–18 minutes or until crispy.

Calories 307, **Fat** (g) 28, **Carbohydrates** (g) 13, **Protein** (g) 4, **Fiber** (g) 3, **Saturated Fat** (g) 4, **Cholesterol** (mg) 0, **Sodium** (mg) 369

ZOOM

You can change the flavor profile of this snack by using a different type of salt. Flavored salts can be found in gourmet shops and, in many cases, in your local supermarket. Go for a lime-infused sea salt or a smoked salt. You can even make your own garlic salt—simply combine 3 parts sea salt with 1 part garlic powder.

Whisking Oil and Vinegar

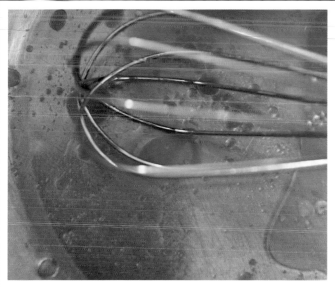

- When you whisk together oil and vinegar vigorously, you create an emulsion.

- The emulsion is temporary, meaning that the two substances will naturally separate.

- So work quickly: Coat the kale leaves as soon as you see the oil and vinegar are blended.

Baking Kale

- The chips will darken a little as they crisp up but should be removed from heat before they brown too much.

- Let the chips cool a little before serving.

CLASSIC BRUSCHETTA

This easy Italian appetizer can be enjoyed at any time of day

Bruschetta (pronounced brus-ketta) is something like an open-faced sandwich of toasted bread topped with, well, any number of things, from cured meats to fresh vegetables and cheese. This classic bruschetta is topped with what is essentially a simple tossed tomato salad.

We've suggested a using a whole wheat baguette. Slice the fresh baguette on an angle about an inch thick, then lightly toast it in a toaster or oven before topping it with the tossed tomatoes. This fresh and summery snack is bursting with color and flavor, not to mention vitamin C and other antioxidants.

Be sure to use ripe plum tomatoes for the recipe. They should be firm, yet leave a print when squeezed.

Yield: 1

Ingredients

3 plum tomatoes, diced

1 tablespoon chopped fresh basil

$^1/_2$ tablespoon olive oil

1 clove garlic, minced

Juice of $^1/_4$ lemon

Sea salt and freshly ground pepper, to taste

2 slices toasted whole wheat baguette

Classic Bruschetta

- In a mixing bowl, toss together the tomatoes, basil, olive oil, garlic, lemon juice, and salt and pepper.

- Serve on the toasted bread.

Calories 238, **Fat** (g) 9, **Carbohydrates** (g) 35, **Protein** (g) 7, **Fiber** (g) 6, **Saturated Fat** (g) 2, **Cholesterol** (mg) 0, **Sodium** (mg) 305

Bruschetta with Avocado: Make the recipe as directed below, except instead of using tomatoes, top your bruschetta with avocado slices. The preparation is simple: Place three slices of freshly cut avocado on the bread and sprinkle with a dash of lemon juice, a dash of balsamic vinegar, a pinch of sea salt, and a pinch of freshly ground pepper.

Olive Tapenade Bruschetta: Top each slice of toasted whole wheat baguette with 1 tablespoon of olive tapenade. Then, add a few slivers of red bell pepper on each surface, and finish with a couple curls of Parmesan cheese.

Chopping Basil

- Before chopping the basil, wash it thoroughly by soaking it in a cold water bath for a few seconds.

- Pat it dry, then remove the leaves from the stems.

- Rock the blade of a sharp chef's knife back and forth over a pile of leaves on a cutting board.

- As the leaves scatter, gather them and continue rocking the knife back and forth over them.

Tossing Ingredients

- Toss the ingredients using salad tongs. Be careful not to bruise or otherwise damage the tomatoes.

- You can also use your (clean!) hands.

CUCUMBER DILL DIP & PITA CHIPS

A dash of dill livens up this tangy cucumber dip

Inspired by Indian and Mediterranean cuisine, this snack combines the refreshing tang of yogurt with the crisp coolness of cucumber and a savory hint of dill.

The expression "cool as a cucumber" is more accurate than you might think. Because cucumbers are mostly water, they can be very hydrating, especially on a hot day or after a workout. They also pack a good dose of fiber, which is important to digestive health. Dill, like parsley, has been shown to help

fight free radicals and carcinogens in the body, such as those that come from smoking or even just grilled foods. It also contains fiber, calcium, and iron.

Yield: 1

Ingredients

1 whole wheat pita, sliced into wedges

1 tablespoon olive oil

1/2 cup plain nonfat Greek yogurt

1/2 cucumber, julienned

1 clove garlic, minced

1 tablespoon chopped fresh dill

Sea salt and freshly ground pepper, to taste

Cucumber Dill Dip & Pita Chips

- Brush the pita wedges with olive oil and place them on a baking sheet.

- In an oven preheated to 400°F, bake them for 10–12 minutes or until crispy.

- In a bowl, combine the other ingredients, mixing well.

- Remove the pita chips from the oven and dip them.

Calories 379, **Fat** (g) 16, **Carbohydrates** (g) 45, **Protein** (g) 13, **Fiber** (g) 2, **Saturated Fat** (g) 2, **Cholesterol** (mg) 7, **Sodium** (mg) 720

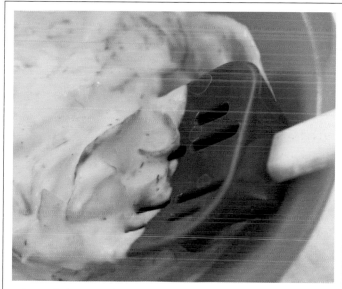

Brushing the Pita

Combining the Ingredients

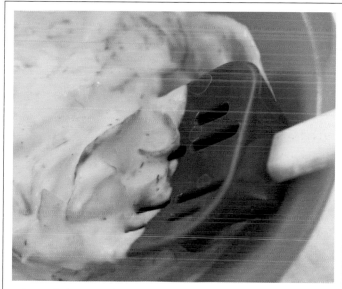

- Brush the pita wedges by dipping just the tip of a basting brush into a small dish containing the oil.

- Then, gently paint on the olive oil.

- You can also use a pump bottle to spray the pita wedges with olive oil.

- Use a fork to mix the ingredients together, but be careful not to damage the cucumber slivers.

BAKED ARTICHOKE DIP & VEGGIES

The heart of the majestic artichoke makes a savory dip

It may look like a flower or cactus in the wild, but the artichoke is actually a perennial thistle. Its outer leaves are tough, and they take a long time to cook. But once you get through to the artichoke's heart, the reward is well worth all the effort.

Artichoke hearts are tender and meaty. They can be steamed, sautéed, or even spread out on a pizza to bake. But artichokes aren't just delicious; they're good for you, too. One artichoke contains about a quarter of the recommended daily intake of fiber for adults, and artichokes are also rich in vitamin C, potassium, folic acid, and magnesium.

Artichoke dip is usually heavy, as it traditionally contains a lot of butter and cheese. This version of the dish makes use of cream cheese and plain nonfat Greek yogurt to achieve the same effect.

Yield: 4 servings

KNACK CALORIE COUNTER COOKBOOK

Ingredients

¹/₂ cup canned artichoke hearts, chopped

¹/₂ cup nonfat cream cheese

¹/₂ cup plain nonfat Greek yogurt

¹/₄ cup low-fat mayonnaise

¹/₄ cup Parmesan cheese, grated

2 cloves garlic, minced

Sea salt and freshly ground pepper, to taste

1 cup carrot and celery sticks

Artichoke Dip & Veggies

- In a mixing bowl, combine all the ingredients.

- Transfer mixture to a small baking dish.

- In an oven preheated to 350°F, bake for 20–25 minutes, or until top starts to brown.

Calories 169, **Fat** (g) 12, **Carbohydrates** (g) 9, **Protein** (g) 8, **Fiber** (g) 2, **Saturated Fat** (g) 5, **Cholesterol** (mg) 23, **Sodium** (mg) 346

Spinach Artichoke Dip: Make the recipe as directed below, but to kick up the flavor, add ½ cup frozen spinach to it. Sauté the spinach with a few drops of water for a few minutes until it melts. Mix the spinach in with the other ingredients, then bake.

Grilled Artichoke Dip: Skewer ½ cup canned artichoke hearts and place them on a hot grill over high heat for 3 minutes on each side or until grill marks appear. Remove from heat and let cool before chopping and adding to other ingredients, as described below.

Chopping Artichoke Hearts

- Make sure the artichokes are chopped finely.
- Using a sharp chef's knife, slice each heart in half, then cut each piece into quarters.

Stirring Ingredients

- To ensure the ingredients get properly combined, whip up the cream cheese, yogurt, and mayonnaise first.
- Then add the other ingredients, mixing well.

SMOOTHIE POPS

Your favorite morning smoothie frozen makes a tasty and refreshing snack

Nothing is more refreshing on a hot day than a frozen treat on a stick. Make your favorite smoothie and freeze it for these tasty smoothie pops. You'll need a freezer pop tray for this recipe. If you don't have one, you can always pour the smoothie mixture into a regular ice cube tray for mini smoothie pops. For the mini versions, you'll be able to enjoy four or five in one serving, depending on the size of the cups in your ice cube tray.

For extra nutrients, fortify your smoothie pops the way you would your morning smoothie. Health food stores carry the types of supplementary ingredients you'll need.

Yield: 2

Ingredients

¹/₂ cup chopped strawberries

¹/₂ cup sliced banana

¹/₂ cup nonfat milk

³/₄ cup orange or apple juice

Smoothie Pops

- In a blender, combine all the ingredients. Blend until smooth.

- Pour the mixture into a freezer pop tray and insert a Popsicle stick into each cup.

- Freeze overnight.

Calories 111, **Fat** (g) 0.5, **Carbohydrates** (g) 24.5, **Protein** (g) 3.5, **Fiber** (g) 2, **Saturated Fat** (g) 0, **Cholesterol** (mg) 1, **Sodium** (mg) 34

Blending the Ingredients

- When blending ice for a regular smoothie, you want to use the pulse setting on the blender.

- Because you'll freeze the smoothie pops, you don't need ice, so blend on high speed.

Inserting the Popsicle Sticks

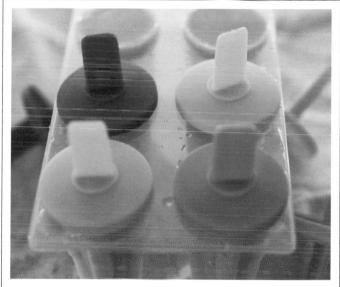

- You can buy Popsicle sticks in most arts and crafts shops, and they may even be available at the supermarket.

- The smoothie will be thick enough that the sticks will stand up on their own.

AFTERNOON SNACKS TO GO

139

BABA GANOUSH & PITA CHIPS

Make your own pita chips to eat with this eggplant-based dip

Bake and mash a large eggplant for this Mediterranean dish. Like most darkly colored fruits and vegetables, bright purple eggplants contain important phytonutrients that work to protect the body's cells from free radicals. Studies have also shown that eating eggplant can reduce cholesterol and improve blood circulation.

Tahini is a paste made of ground sesame seeds. It can be used as an alternative to butter or margarine in cooking and as a spread, and it is an important ingredient in many popular Middle Eastern recipes. Sesame seeds are rich in copper, magnesium, and calcium, the latter of which is important to digestive and bone health.

Yield: 2

KNACK CALORIE COUNTER COOKBOOK

Ingredients

1 small whole wheat pita, sliced into wedges

1 large eggplant, halved

Juice of $1/4$ lemon

1 clove garlic, minced

1 tablespoon tahini

1 tablespoon plus 1 teaspoon olive oil

2 tablespoons finely chopped fresh parsley

Sea salt, to taste

Calories 200, **Fat** (g) 11, **Carbohydrates** (g) 24, **Protein** (g) 5, **Fiber** (g) 9, **Saturated Fat** (g) 2, **Cholesterol** (mg) 0, **Sodium** (mg) 3574

Baba Ganoush & Pita Chips

- Brush the pita wedges with the teaspoon of olive oil and place them on a baking sheet.

- In an oven preheated to 400°F, bake them for 10–12 minutes or until crispy.

- Bake the eggplant. Combine the flesh with the lemon juice, garlic, tahini, and tablespoon of olive oil and blend. Stir in parsley and salt and serve.

Spicy Baba Ganoush: Kick up your eggplant dip with a touch of heat. Prepare it as described below, except add 1 teaspoon of chopped chile peppers to the mixture. You can use guajillo peppers or even chipotle in adobo sauce.

Minty Baba Ganoush: Prepare your baba ganoush as described below, but add a splash of color and freshness to the dip by tossing 1 tablespoon finely chopped fresh mint into the eggplant mixture. Blend until well incorporated and smooth. Garnish the final result with a sprig of fresh mint.

Baking Eggplant

- After baking the pita chips, leave the oven at 400°F to bake the eggplant.

- Place the eggplant halves cut side down in a baking dish, and bake until tender, about 30 minutes.

Preparing Baba Ganoush

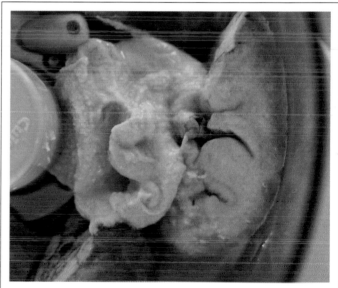

- Remove the eggplant from the oven and scoop out the flesh.

- In a blender, combine the eggplant flesh with the lemon juice, garlic, tahini, and olive oil, and blend until smooth.

- Allow the mixture to cool before stirring in the parsley and salt.

- Serve with the pita chips.

AFTERNOON SNACKS TO GO

EDAMAME

Serve these soybeans as you would a bowl of nuts or olives—simply

Soy is the most widely grown and used legume in the world—not only because people consume it, but also because so much of the livestock we raise eats it.

For people, soy has become a popular replacement for those who prefer not to eat meat or who simply have cut back their meat intake, because it's so high in protein but relatively low in saturated fat. Studies have shown that eating soy can help people reduce or keep off weight because

it causes us to produce smaller fat cells. More importantly, eating soy has been shown to help reduce bad cholesterol levels and regulate blood pressure.

Yield: 1

Ingredients

1 cup fresh or frozen edamame (soybeans), in shells

Sea salt, to taste

Edamame

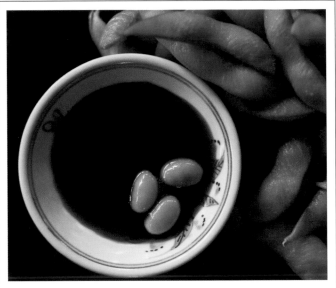

- Over high heat, bring a pot of water to a boil.

- Toss in the edamame and reduce heat.

- Allow the edamame to simmer for a minute or two, then drain and season.

- If using frozen, let the edamame simmer a minute or two longer.

Calories 240, **Fat** (g) 10, **Carbohydrates** (g) 16, **Protein** (g) 20, **Fiber** (g) 10, **Saturated Fat** (g) 0, **Cholesterol** (mg) 0, **Sodium** (mg) 830

Draining Edamame

Popping Edamame Open

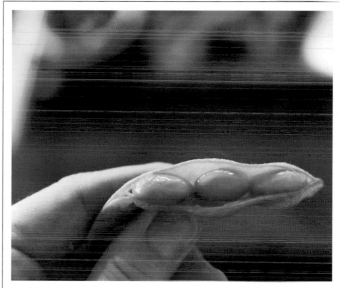

- Remove the edamame from heat and drain by pouring into a colander.

- It's a good idea to rinse the edamame with cold water immediately so that they stop cooking.

- To enjoy edamame, use your teeth and lips to squeeze the beans out of the shells.

- The shells are salted, but you don't eat them. Just suck on them, then suck out the beans.

- Most pods contain three beans.

TRAIL MIX

Take trail mix on long or active outings to keep your energy up

Trail mix is a hiker's best friend. If you enjoy long walks—whether it's up a mountain, along the beach, or even through the mall—take a small bag of trail mix to nibble on throughout your outing.

Nuts may be high in fat, but they contain good fats that actually help to reverse the effects of bad fats, lowering LDL or "bad cholesterol."

Dried fruits are little concentrated versions of fresh fruits, high in fiber to help your body digest. Mini semisweet chocolate chips add a little touch of sweetness to the crunch and chewiness of the nuts and dried fruit. They also add a little dose of antioxidants to your snack to keep your immune system strong.

Yield: 12 servings

Ingredients

¹/₂ cup dried cranberries

¹/₂ cup dried apple pieces

¹/₂ cup dried apricots

¹/₂ cup banana chips

¹/₂ cup dried blueberries

¹/₂ cup unsalted peanuts

¹/₂ cup raw cashews

¹/₂ cup raw almonds

¹/₂ cup pumpkin seeds

¹/₂ cup shelled sunflower seeds

¹/₄ cup mini semisweet chocolate chips

Trail Mix

- Combine all the ingredients in a large bowl.
- Serve from the bowl, or store individual servings in 12 sandwich bags.

Calories 284, **Fat** (g) 19, **Carbohydrates** (g) 25, **Protein** (g) 7, **Fiber** (g) 4, **Saturated Fat** (g) 4, **Cholesterol** (mg) 1, **Sodium** (mg) 10

Trail Mix with Yogurt Chips: Trail mix is one of those snacks that can really incorporate anything you like or happen to have lying around the pantry. Instead of chocolate chips, toss in ¼ cup yogurt chips to add an extra touch of sweetness to this snack.

Goji Berry Trail Mix: Up the nutritional value of your trail mix with the latest fruit being touted a superfood. Goji berries are said to protect the liver, improve eyesight, promote healthy circulation and boost immunity. Add ½ cup to your mix for good measure.

The Ingredients

- Dried fruits contain some of the nutrients of the original fresh versions, but many of the nutrients get lost as the fruits dry.

- Still, dried fruits provide some of the fiber, vitamin A, beta-carotene, and potassium of the original fruits.

- One portion of the trail mix is equal to just under ½ cup.

Storing Trail Mix

- Keep individual servings in separate sandwich bags to take on the go.

- You can also store individual servings in sealable plastic containers.

AFTERNOON SNACKS TO GO

GLAZED NUTS

Add a touch of honey and spice to nuts for an irresistible snack

Eating nuts, which contain monounsaturated fats (the kind that can help reverse the effects of saturated and trans fats), is recommended as part of a healthy diet. Walnuts, in particular, have been shown to lower cholesterol, improve cardiovascular function, lower the risk of heart disease, control high blood pressure, and improve brain function. Not bad for a little nut.

For this recipe, we use raw walnuts, but you can incorporate nearly any of your favorite nuts. In fact, using a combination of different nuts—each with their own flavors and textures—will make for a more exciting snack.

Yield: 2

Ingredients

1 cup raw walnuts

1 tablespoon honey

¹/₂ teaspoon vanilla

Pinch of cinnamon

Pinch of sea salt

Calories 362, **Fat** (g) 32, **Carbohydrates** (g) 16, **Protein** (g) 8, **Fiber** (g) 4, **Saturated Fat** (g) 4, **Cholesterol** (mg) 0, **Sodium** (mg) 2

Glazed Nuts

- In a mixing bowl, toss together all the ingredients and mix so that the nuts are well coated.

- Line a cookie sheet with parchment, and spread the nuts out on the sheet.

- In an oven heated to 250°F, bake for 10–15 minutes, turning every 10 minutes.

- Allow the nuts to cool before serving or storing.

Use your leftover Glazed Nuts as toppings for any number of desserts. Sprinkle a handful of them onto a couple scoops of plain frozen yogurt for an added crunch and touch of sweetness, or use a few teaspoons of them to garnish cakes and muffins, and at the same time up their protein content.

Assorted Glazed Nuts: Instead of just walnuts, use pecans, almonds, or a combination of all three. Toss in some hazelnuts for extra crunch and depth of flavor. You can also toss in cashews, which contain less fat than other types of nut.

Tossing Ingredients

Spreading on Cookie Sheet

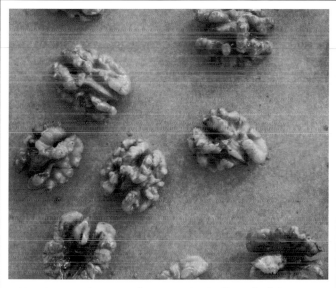

- To toss the ingredients, use a spatula or wooden spoon.
- You may want to lightly spray your spatula or wooden spoon with oil to prevent the nut mixture from sticking to it.

- Use the spatula or wooden spoon to spread the nuts on the parchment-lined cookie sheet.
- Again, if you find the nut mixture is sticking to your utensil, lightly spray it with oil.

GUACAMOLE & TORTILLA CHIPS

This Mexican avocado dip is a great snack for parties or if you're flying solo

Guacamole is the perfect party snack, but you can also enjoy this creamy avocado dip on your own. Depending on how chunky you like your guacamole, you can modify the degree to which you mash the avocados and how finely you chop the other ingredients.

Yes, avocadoes are high in fat. With 30 grams of fat per fruit, one avocado contains as much fat as a burger. But fear not: there are different types of fats and they have different effects on the body. Much of the fat in avocadoes is monounsaturated, which can reverse the effects of bad fats. So, enjoy avocadoes in moderation. You can even use this guacamole to replace mayo or other sandwich spreads. *Yield: 2*

Ingredients

2 ripe avocados

1/2 onion, diced

1 clove garlic, minced

Juice of 1/2 lemon

1/4 cup finely chopped fresh cilantro

Sea salt and freshly ground pepper

2 ounces baked tortilla chips

Guacamole & Tortilla Chips

- In a bowl, mash the avocados using a fork or potato masher.

- Combine with onion, garlic, lemon juice, cilantro, and salt and pepper, mixing well.

- Serve with chips.

Calories 408, **Fat** (g) 33, **Carbohydrates** (g) 30.5, **Protein** (g) 5.5, **Fiber** (g) 14.5, **Saturated Fat** (g) 4.5, **Cholesterol** (mg) 0, **Sodium** (mg) 230

Chunky Guacamole: Add tomato to your avocado dip to make it chunkier, and you'll also be getting an extra dose of vitamin C in your snack. Seed and finely dice a ripe plum tomato. Add the tomato to the mashed avocado with the other ingredients. Mix together well.

Spicy Guacamole: Kick up the spice in your guacamole with a chopped jalapeno pepper. Seed and finely dice a fresh jalapeno, and add it to the avocado mash along with the other ingredients. Mix it in well.

Pitting Avocados

- Use a sharp chef's knife to slice the avocado in half lengthwise, cutting around the pit.

- Separate the two halves and hold the side containing the pit in your palm.

- With your knife, carefully but firmly strike the pit of the avocado, hard enough for the knife to become stuck in the pit.

- Hold the avocado as you twist the pit using the knife as a handle. It should pop right out.

Combining the Ingredients

- Use a fork to mix together the ingredients.

- The lemon juice will help prevent the avocados from turning brown from oxidation, so add it to the mash first.

- Feel free to add more or less lemon juice, onion, or cilantro based on your personal taste.

WHOLE ROAST CHICKEN
Garlic and rosemary infuse this whole chicken with flavor

Knowing how to roast a chicken is one of those basic skills everyone should have. Start by making sure your chicken is clean. Rinse it under cold water, inside and out, then pat it dry using a paper towel.

For this recipe, we stuff the cavity with garlic and rosemary, which saturate the entire bird with a savory, herbaceous flavor. Rub both the inside and outside of the chicken with olive oil to moisten the skin and keep the juices sealed inside.

A little salt and pepper are all the extra seasoning that is needed. Then, we truss it to keep all the juicy flavors inside. *Yield: 6*

Ingredients

1 3-4 pound whole chicken

$1/4$ cup olive oil

Sea salt and freshly ground pepper, to taste

5 cloves garlic, smashed

2 sprigs of rosemary

Calories 223, **Fat** (g) 14, **Carbohydrates** (g) 1, **Protein** (g) 21, **Fiber** (g) 0, **Saturated Fat** (g) 3, **Cholesterol** (mg) 65, **Sodium** (mg) 64

Whole Roast Chicken

- Remove the giblets from the cavity of the chicken, and trim any excess fat.

- Rinse the chicken and pat it dry using a paper towel.

- Coat the chicken with olive oil, then salt and pepper it. Stuff the cavity with the garlic and rosemary. Truss the chicken.

- Cook, covered in foil, in a preheated 450°F oven for 1¼ hours. Remove foil for the last 10 minutes of cooking.

Lemon-infused Roast Chicken: For a little extra refreshing zest, add a whole quartered lemon to the cavity of the chicken when you stuff it. Prepare the chicken as described below, and when you stuff the cavity with garlic and rosemary, add the lemon wedges.

Spicy Roast Chicken: Prepare the chicken as described below. Only, when you season it, instead of just salt and pepper, combine 1 teaspoon salt with pinches black pepper, paprika, cayenne pepper, dried basil, and cumin. Sprinkle the spice blend evenly all over the chicken, inside and out.

Preparing the Chicken

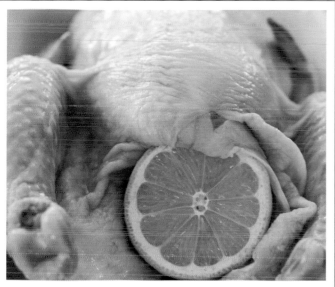

- Once the giblets are removed, coat the inside and outside of the chicken with the olive oil.

- Salt and pepper the chicken, inside and outside.

- Place the chicken in a medium-size roasting pan.

- Stuff the cavity with the lemon, garlic, and rosemary. Then truss the chicken.

Trussing the Chicken

- To truss the chicken, run a string around the back of the bird, up and over the thighs, and under and around the wings. Then tie it around the end of the legs to close the cavity.

- Once the chicken is stuffed and trussed, cover it loosely with tinfoil.

- In an oven preheated to 450°F, roast the chicken for 1¼ hours or about 20 minutes per pound. Remove the foil for the last 10 minutes of cooking.

- Allow it to cool for a few minutes before removing the string, carving, and serving.

LEISURELY DINNER

HOT & SOUR PORK TENDERLOIN

This Asian-inspired pork tenderloin is sure to please

Tenderloin is such an overlooked cut of meat. As lean as the leanest cut of chicken, yet full of flavor, it's perfect for marinating or simple cooking with a little salt and pepper.

A combination of sweet, sour, and spicy flavors makes this pork tenderloin dish a winner. It's best enjoyed a little pink in the middle.

The pork is sweetened with hoisin sauce, also called "suckling pig sauce," a concoction of sugar, soybeans, white distilled vinegar, rice, salt, flour, garlic, and red chile peppers used in Chinese cooking.

You can also kick up the heat in this recipe by tossing in some hot peppers. A little spice can be nice!
Yield: 5

Ingredients

1/4 cup olive oil

3 tablespoons soy sauce

3 tablespoons hoisin sauce

2 tablespoons hot mustard

Juice of 1/2 lime

2 cloves garlic, minced

2 tablespoons grated fresh ginger

1 1-pound pork tenderloin

1 yellow bell pepper, roughly chopped

1 red bell pepper, roughly chopped

Calories 247, **Fat** (g) 14, **Carbohydrates** (g) 12, **Protein** (g) 19, **Fiber** (g) 2, **Saturated Fat** (g) 2, **Cholesterol** (mg) 52, **Sodium** (mg) 1095

Hot & Sour Pork Tenderloin

- In a shallow bowl, combine the olive oil, soy sauce, hoisin sauce, hot mustard, lime juice, garlic, and ginger, and whisk together until smooth.

- Marinate the tenderloin in this mixture for 20 minutes or more.

- In a large pan over medium-high heat, sear the tenderloin on each side for 5–6 minutes.

- Arrange the bell peppers around the tenderloin and, in an oven preheated to 375°F, cook for 15–18 minutes, or until a little pink inside.

• • • • RECIPE VARIATION • • • •

Spicy Pork Tenderloin: Kick up the spice in this dish by adding a single Thai pepper to it. Seed and slice it lengthwise, then sauté it for a few minutes before adding it to the rest of the ingredients for the marinade, as described below.

Marinating Tenderloin

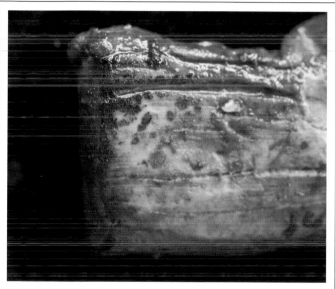

Slicing Tenderloin

- Rinse off the tenderloin and pat it dry before placing it in the bowl to marinate.

- Ensure that the marinade covers the tenderloin completely.

- Allow it to marinate for 20 minutes or more in the fridge.

- Remove the tenderloin from its marinade.

- Remove the tenderloin from the pan and place it on a cutting board to cool.

- Slice it diagonally and serve 2–3 slices per person with the peppers over the top.

ARCTIC CHAR WITH FENNEL
A subtle hint of anise brings this simple fish dish to life

Arctic char is a species of fish related to both salmon and trout. Found in both fresh water and saltwater, it's one of the species of fish harvested in an environmentally sustainable way. In other words, like certain types of salmon and tuna, Arctic char are not being overfished.

Like salmon, Arctic char contains omega-3 fatty acids, which help prevent cardiovascular disease and lower blood pressure.

Fennel also boasts some important health benefits. Used as both a vegetable and an herb, it's high in iron and can help soothe indigestion and other digestive issues, from constipation to its direct opposite!
Yield: 1

Ingredients

¹/₂ bulb fennel, sliced

¹/₂ red onion, sliced

3 tablespoons olive oil

Juice of ¹/₂ lemon, divided

Sea salt and freshly ground pepper, to taste

1 4-ounce Arctic char fillet

Calories 585, **Fat** (g) 49, **Carbohydrates** (g) 11, **Protein** (g) 24, **Fiber** (g) 4, **Saturated Fat** (g) 7, **Cholesterol** (mg) 27, **Sodium** (mg) 535

Arctic Char with Fennel

- Place the fennel and onion in a baking dish.

- Coat the fennel and onion with the olive oil, half of the lemon juice, and a sprinkle of salt and pepper.

- In a preheated 400°F oven, roast the veggies for 10–15 minutes.

- Season the fish with salt, pepper and lemon and add it to the baking dish. Cook for 20 minutes or until done.

Arctic Char with More Fennel: For an extra burst of color and flavor, use the leaves of the fennel to add to your fish. Remove the leaves as you prepare the fennel. Wash and pat them dry, then finely chop them. Add them to the fish near the end of cooking.

Arctic Char with Potatoes: Make this dish more substantial by adding new potatoes to the mix. Quarter four or five baby potatoes, leaving the skins on. As you coat the fennel and onion in olive oil and seasonings, do the same to the potatoes, then add them to the baking dish with the other veggies as described below.

Prepare the Fish

- While the veggies are roasting, rinse and pat dry the fish.

- Sprinkle it with salt and pepper.

- Squeeze the other half of the lemon juice onto the fish.

Baking the Fish

- Take the baking dish out of the oven.

- Move the veggies to the sides and place the fish at the center of the baking dish.

- Return the dish to the oven and continue cooking for another 20 minutes, or until the fish is cooked through.

BEEF & BROCCOLI STIR-FRY

This hearty stir-fry packs a nutritional punch with iron-rich beef and broccoli

The two main ingredients in this dish are both good sources of iron, which makes this an excellent meal to have if you're fighting off a feeling of low energy.

Of course, broccoli, like all cruciferous vegetables, is not only high in iron, but also in cancer-fighting antioxidants. Beef, however, gets a mixed report card. For this dish, use sirloin or another type of loin. Other lean cuts of beef include anything with "round" in the name. A 3-ounce portion of lean beef is a good source of iron, protein, and zinc. Just be sure to trim away excess fat when preparing any cut of beef.

Yield: 4 servings

Ingredients

3 tablespoons vegetable oil, divided

³/₄ pound boneless sirloin, cut into ¹/₄-inch-thick slices

Sea salt and freshly ground pepper

3 cloves garlic, minced

1 tablespoon grated fresh ginger

3 tablespoons soy sauce

1 tablespoon honey

1 pound broccoli, cut into florets, stems peeled and cubed

Calories 445, **Fat** (g) 22, **Carbohydrates** (g) 35, **Protein** (g) 28, **Fiber** (g) 5, **Saturated Fat** (g) 5, **Cholesterol** (mg) 66, **Sodium** (mg) 958

Beef & Broccoli Stir-Fry

- In a wok or large nonstick pan, heat up 1 tablespoon of the oil over medium-high. Toss in the sirloin slices.

- Sprinkle with salt and pepper and stir-fry for 5–10 minutes.

- Remove the beef from the wok.

- Add the rest of the oil and toss in the garlic, ginger, soy sauce, honey, and broccoli. Stir-fry for 12–15 minutes.

- Toss the beef back in and stir-fry until the meat is cooked through.

- Serve over brown rice or rice noodles.

Sesame Stir-fry: To add a hint of a nutty flavor, as well as a shot of calcium and extra fiber to your dish, add 1 teaspoon of sesame seeds to it. Prepare the stir-fry as described below, then sprinkle the seeds on as a garnish at the end. They not only look pretty, but pack a taste and nutritional punch.

Chicken Broccoli Stir-fry: You can make this stir-fry with chicken. Use ¾ pound boneless, skinless lean chicken breast, sliced into bite-sized pieces. Par-cook it as you would the sirloin, then remove it from the wok to cook the broccoli, and return it to the wok to cook it through.

Heating Wok with Oil

- When stir-frying, you want your wok or pan to already be hot before you add anything to it.

- Heat up your oil by itself for a minute or so, being careful not to let it get to the point of smoking.

- For this recipe, add the other seasonings before adding the broccoli. Use a wooden spoon to stir what's frying.

Broccoli and Beef Frying

- Use store-bought grated ginger or grate your own from the root.

- To ensure the right texture and appearance of the beef, par cook it, then remove it to cook the broccoli.

- Stir-frying meat with vegetables can lead to the meat becoming soggy from the moisture of the vegetables.

- Separating the two will allow the meat to brown nicely.

LEISURELY DINNER

MUSHROOM & EDAMAME RISOTTO

The key to any risotto is all in the wrist . . . stir, stir, stir

Making risotto is not difficult, but does require a diligent attention to detail. The consistency of the rice is constantly changing and thickening. To avoid burning the rice, you must stir constantly.

This dish incorporates edamame, or soybeans, which are rich in protein and have been deemed a superfood by some nutrition experts. Studies show that consuming soy can help lower LDL cholesterol and blood pressure. It's also been said

that soybeans can help us stay lean, as they contain compounds that cause us to produce smaller fat cells.

As with all risottos, the key to this one is the strong tangy Parmesan cheese, which not only flavors the dish but gives it the right creamy consistency.

Yield: 2

Ingredients

1 tablespoon olive oil

1 clove garlic, minced

¼ pound fresh mushrooms, sliced (porcini, chanterelles, or morels)

1 cup Arborio rice

½ cup dry white wine or fino sherry

3 cups vegetable stock

¼ pound fresh edamame (soybeans)

1 ounce grated Parmesan cheese

Sea salt and freshly ground pepper, to taste

Calories 633, **Fat** (g) 16, **Carbohydrates** (g) 89, **Protein** (g) 15, **Fiber** (g) 4, **Saturated Fat** (g) 3, **Cholesterol** (mg) 12, **Sodium** (mg) 852

Mushroom & Edamame Risotto

- In a saucepan over medium-high heat, heat up the oil.

- Add the garlic and mushrooms, and fry for a few minutes, until the mushrooms soften.

- Gradually add the rice, wine, and stock. Allow the liquid to absorb and the rice to cook, then stir in the edamame, cheese, and salt and pepper.

It Doesn't Have to Be Arborio: Arborio rice is one of the best to use when making risotto, but there are other short-grained round varieties native to Italy that also work. Try Vialone Nano or Carnaroli. All are grown in the Po Valley, near Venetia.

Mushroom & Asparagus Risotto: Replace the soybeans in this recipe with ¼ pound chopped asparagus tips. This natural diuretic is high in folate, a nutrient that is essential to our cardiovascular health. Prepare the risotto as described below, except add the asparagus to the saucepan when you cook the mushrooms and garlic to soften them. Then, add the rice and proceed as outlined.

Adding Ingredients

- First add the rice. Allow it to fry for a few minutes, until it starts to brown.

- Next, add the wine and stir.

- Allow the wine to reach a simmer before starting to add the stock, little by little, stirring frequently.

Stirring the Risotto

- Keep the risotto at a simmer as you stir intermittently, never letting the rice dry out and continuing to add more stock as needed.

- Once all the liquid is absorbed and the rice has reached a creamy texture, stir in the edamame, Parmesan, and as much salt and pepper as desired.

LEISURELY DINNER

ROASTED VEGETABLE CURRY

Make this curry as spicy—or not—as you like

The spices in this dish pack little nutrient punches. Curry powder is actually a blend of several of the other spices in the dish. It usually contains turmeric, cumin, cardamom, and coriander. We add more turmeric to this dish to accentuate its flavor and color, and we get extra health-promoting benefits in the process, such as its liver detoxifying and anti-inflammation properties. We also add more cumin, which is good for digestion.

If you tend to shy away from spices, this dish is a great way to be reintroduced to them. The yogurt adds a creaminess to the dish that softens the heat. Dairy, after all, is the best way to put out a fire in your mouth.

Yield: 3–4 servings

Ingredients

1 small head cauliflower, cut into florets

2 carrots, sliced

3 red potatoes, unpeeled, cleaned and cubed

3 tablespoons olive oil, divided

Sea salt and freshly ground pepper, to taste

2 tablespoons curry powder

Pinch of turmeric

Pinch of cumin

Pinch of cinnamon

1 tablespoon tomato paste

3 cloves garlic, minced

1 red chile, seeded and finely chopped

2 shallots, chopped

1/4 cup plain nonfat yogurt

1/4 cup finely chopped cilantro

1/2 cup fresh or frozen peas

1 teaspoon grated fresh ginger

2 cups Basmati rice

Calories 581, **Fat** (g) 15, **Carbohydrates** (g) 102, **Protein** (g) 15, **Fiber** (g) 11, **Saturated Fat** (g) 1, **Cholesterol** (mg) 1, **Sodium** (mg) 355

Roasted Vegetable Curry

- Place the cauliflower, carrots, and potatoes in a roasting pan and coat well with 2 tablespoons of the olive oil.

- Toss the vegetables with salt and pepper.

- Place the pan in an oven preheated to 400°F.

- Roast the vegetables for 25–30 minutes, stirring once or twice.

- Heat up the rest of the ingredients and add to the veggies. Serve over rice.

Heating the Other Ingredients

Finishing the Curry

- In a saucepan over medium heat, heat up the remaining 1 tablespoon of oil.

- Add the dried spices, tomato paste, garlic, chile, ginger and shallots.

- Stir until ingredients are well blended and the shallots are soft.

- Reduce the heat, then add the roasted vegetables. Stir to coat well.

- Add the yogurt, cilantro, and peas and continue stirring for another 15–20 minutes over low heat.

- Serve over basmati rice.

LEISURELY DINNER

161

QUICK SHRIMP STIR-FRY
Use fresh or frozen jumbo shrimp for this easy stir-fry

The key to this quick and easy stir-fry is exactly that—it's quick! The shrimp cooks up in minutes, and the sugar snap peas are best enjoyed al dente. To avoid overcooking the shrimp, keep close watch on its color. As soon as the shrimp has completely changed from bluish-gray to pink, it is done. You want the texture to be snappy—overcooked shrimp will be more on the tough, rubbery side, and it loses some of its flavor.

Shrimp isn't just a great source of protein; it's also high in vitamin D and vitamin B$_{12}$, two nutrients essential to our cellular health.

Yield: 2 servings

Ingredients

1 tablespoon olive oil

3 cloves garlic, minced

1/2 pound jumbo shrimp, cleaned and deveined

Juice of 1/2 lemon

Sea salt and freshly ground pepper, to taste

1/2 pound sugar snap peas, rinsed, ends chopped off

1/3 cup brown rice or rice noodles, cooked

1/4 cup finely chopped fresh thyme

Quick Shrimp Stir-fry

Calories 232, **Fat** (g) 9, **Carbohydrates** (g) 12, **Protein** (g) 25, **Fiber** (g) 4, **Saturated Fat** (g) 1, **Cholesterol** (mg) 162, **Sodium** (mg) 396

- Heat oil in a wok or skillet over medium-high heat. Add garlic and sauté for a minute or less before adding shrimp. Be sure not to let garlic brown.

- Pour in lemon juice and sprinkle in salt and pepper, stirring intermittently.

- After 5–8 minutes, when the shrimp are starting to turn pink, toss in sugar snap peas and thyme.

- Continue to stir for another 5–8 minutes for al dente peas, or longer if you prefer them softer. Serve over 1/3 cup brown rice or rice noodles.

Bigger Shrimp Stir-fry: We recommend using jumbo shrimp. You can go extra jumbo or colossal on the shrimp if you like; just use fewer of them. If you buy shrimp with the heads still on, cook them that way, as they keep the flavors and juices of the meat sealed in better.

Shrimp & Green Bean Stir-fry: Instead of sugar snap peas, you can use garden variety green beans. Prepare the recipe as is described below, except replace the sugar snap peas with ½ green beans, chopped into 1½-inch long pieces.

Chopping off Ends of Peas

- Sugar snap peas require very little prep work.

- Simply rinse them under cold water in a colander.

- Place the peas on a chopping block and, using a sharp chef's knife, slice both ends off each pod.

- Be careful not to slice too far up the pod, or you'll cut into the peas themselves.

Deveining Shrimp

- The black "vein" that runs along the back of the shrimp is actually its digestive tract.

- It's edible, but if the idea of it is unappealing to you, you can remove it.

- Take a sharp paring knife and run it along the line where the vein is, splitting open the skin. Rinse out the grit inside under cold water.

- Only devein larger shrimp. The smaller ones are too much hassle and the vein is barely noticeable.

QUICK DINNER

SAUSAGE WITH ONIONS & PEPPERS

This easy take on an Italian classic uses turkey sausage instead of traditional pork

For our twist on this classic Italian recipe, we're using turkey sausages instead of the usual spicy pork. Spicy Italian-style turkey sausages are available in many grocery stores. Turkey is leaner than pork sausage, with not only fewer calories, but also less fat.

If you can't find spicy Italian sausages, especially ones made with turkey instead of pork, you can always buy regular or sweet turkey sausages and add the spice to the dish yourself. You'll want to add fennel and a healthy dose of hot paprika to the dish. If you can't find hot paprika, you can always substitute cayenne pepper.

Yield: 2 servings

Ingredients

1 tablespoon olive oil, divided

4 spicy Italian-style turkey sausages, roughly 1 pound

2 cloves garlic, minced

1 yellow onion, chopped

Sea salt and freshly ground pepper, to taste

1 red bell pepper, chopped

1 yellow bell pepper, chopped

2 bay leaves

Pinch of oregano

Calories 285, **Fat** (g) 17, **Carbohydrates** (g) 16, **Protein** (g) 19, **Fiber** (g) 3, **Saturated Fat** (g) 5, **Cholesterol** (mg) 59, **Sodium** (mg) 1353

Sausage with Onions and Peppers

- Heat up oiled pan over medium-high heat. Sear sausages on all sides for a few minutes each.

- Place sausages in a baking dish and cook 10–15 minutes in a 350ºF preheated oven.

- Heat up the rest of the oil and add the garlic, onions, and salt and pepper. Sauté until onions are soft.

- Toss in peppers, bay leaves, and oregano and sauté another 5–8 minutes, until peppers have softened. Transfer sausages to the pan and cook 10 minutes, stirring once.

Sausage & Peppers Sandwich: Turn this dish into a satisfying sandwich by taking the sausages from the baking dish and letting them cool enough to slice them on an angle into bite-sized pieces. Return the sliced sausage to the pan with the peppers and finish cooking through. Spoon some of the sausage and peppers onto half a whole wheat baguette, and serve.

Sausage & Peppers Pasta: This recipe also works well as a pasta dish. Cook 8 ounces of your favorite noodles until al dente. Slice up the par-cooked sausages, then toss them with the sautéed onions and peppers, and cooked pasta (roughly 4 cups). Shave a little Parmesan onto each portion, and serve.

Chopping Veggies

- Slice your peppers into strips.

- Start by chopping off each end of the pepper, then cut it in half.

- Seed the pepper, then proceed to slice each half into strips.

Cooking Sausages

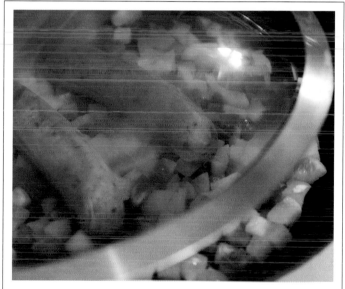

- If you're using an oven-friendly pan, such as a cast-iron skillet, you can skip the step of transferring the sausages to a baking dish.

- Instead, simply transfer the skillet to the preheated oven.

QUICK DINNER

POTATO & ZUCCHINI FRITTATA
This Italian-style omelet is baked, not fried

A frittata is an Italian version of an omelet. Whereas an omelet is fried, a frittata is traditionally partially fried and partially broiled. In this recipe, we bake the frittata like a quiche.

Frittatas, like omelets and quiches, can incorporate any combination of vegetables, meats, and cheeses you wish. In Italy, they sometimes even include pasta—essentially, whatever leftovers are in the fridge can be tossed in.

For this frittata, we're using potatoes and zucchini. The potatoes give density to the dish, to ensure that you feel full after eating it! Yet, the zucchini give it a light freshness, especially where they're cooked just al dente.

Yield: 2 servings

Ingredients

2 red potatoes, unpeeled, cleaned and cubed

1 tablespoon olive oil

Sea salt and freshly ground pepper, to taste

2 eggs plus 4 egg whites

1/3 cup nonfat milk

1 shallot, chopped

1 clove garlic, minced

1/4 cup finely chopped fresh tarragon

1 zucchini, unpeeled, sliced

1 ounce freshly grated Parmesan cheese

Calories 422, **Fat** (g) 17, **Carbohydrates** (g) 43, **Protein** (g) 26, **Fiber** (g) 5, **Saturated Fat** (g) 5, **Cholesterol** (mg) 225, **Sodium** (mg) 597

Potato and Zucchini Frittata

- In a nonstick baking dish, combine potatoes, olive oil, and salt and pepper, coating potatoes well.

- In a 375°F preheated oven, cook potatoes for 15 minutes. While potatoes cook, combine eggs, milk, shallots, garlic, and tarragon in a mixing bowl, whisking well.

- Remove potatoes from the oven and layer zucchini over top. Pour egg mixture over the zucchini and potatoes.

- Sprinkle Parmesan over top and bake at 400°F 15–20 minutes, or until set. Allow the frittata to cool for a few minutes before serving.

166

Mixed Veggie & Chicken Frittata: Instead of using potatoes and zucchini, toss in ½ cup chopped bell peppers, ½ cup chopped onions, and ½ cup cubed cooked chicken. Tomatoes, Asiago cheese, and cubed baked ham are another great combination for this dish.

Herbed Frittata: You can also change the flavors of this dish by changing the herbs used. Instead of tarragon, toss in ¼ cup finely chopped fresh basil leaves or oregano. The fresh herbs add a touch of color and a nutritional boost to the frittata.

Grating Parmesan

- Using fresh Parmesan will impart much more intense flavors to your dish.

- To grate the Parmesan, run the wedge of cheese back and forth over a grater set over a bowl. Watch the shreds of cheese drop into the bowl below.

- Alternatively, use a potato peeler to shave curls of cheese from the wedge.

- Sprinkle the grated cheese over the zucchini right before putting the dish in the oven.

Pouring Eggs over Potatoes

- Remove the potatoes from the oven and allow the baking dish to cool for several minutes.

- Then spray the dish with a bit more olive oil and pour the egg mixture over the potatoes.

- Alternatively, you can transfer your potatoes to a new prepared baking dish.

QUICK DINNER

WHITE PIZZA

This delicate version of a pizza pie looks as good as it tastes

Traditionally, a pizza pie has three key ingredients: the dough, the cheese, and the tomato sauce. We omit the sauce for this light, cheesy white pizza. Versions of white pizza can be found in Rome and New York, although this version is definitely New York–style. The red sauce is replaced with a garlicky, creamy white sauce. Usually, this white sauce is butter-based, but we've used olive oil, skim milk, white wine, and ricotta cheese to achieve an effect that is just as satisfying.

Serve this light white pizza with a simple salad of mesclun spritzed with a little olive oil and balsamic vinegar.
Yield: 1 12-inch pizza (2 servings)

KNACK CALORIE COUNTER COOKBOOK

Ingredients

12 ounces whole wheat pizza dough (recipe follows)

1 tablespoon olive oil, divided

1/2 yellow onion, diced

2 cloves garlic, minced

1/4 cup white wine

1/4 cup nonfat milk

Pinch of dried thyme

Pinch of dried oregano

Pinch of dried basil

3/4 cup low-fat ricotta

Sea salt and freshly ground pepper, to taste

For the dough:

1 1/2 teaspoons instant yeast

3/4 cup warm water

1 1/2 cups white whole wheat flour

1 tablespoon olive oil

1 teaspoon honey

1/2 teaspoon salt

Calories 622, Fat (g) 23, Carbohydrates (g) 80, Protein (g) 26, Fiber (g) 12, Saturated Fat (g) 7, Cholesterol (mg) 29, Sodium (mg) 955

White Pizza

- Combine yeast and 1/4 cup of water; let stand until it fizzes.

- Combine the rest of the ingredients in a mixing bowl, and add yeast mixture. Mix well, using your hands or an electric mixer. Add extra flour if dough is too sticky.

- Shape pizza dough and place it on a pizza stone or dusted baking sheet. Brush with sauce, then spread ricotta over the top. Sprinkle with salt and pepper.

- In a 500°F preheated oven, bake pizza 12 minutes, or until top bubbles.

Broccoli Pizza: Vegetables on a pizza may be sacrilege to some. But try this recipe with tiny broccoli florets and you'll surely love it. Take a head of broccoli and chop it into tiny, bite-size florets, discarding the stems. Place the florets on the pizza before it goes into the oven. Brush them with olive oil so they crisp slightly as you bake the pizza.

A Different Kind of Margherita: Margherita pizza is traditionally topped with marinara sauce, buffalo mozzarella, and fresh basil. Using the same color scheme, we've come up with a different red-green-and-white pizza. Prepare the white pizza as described below, but top with 1 cup sliced red bell peppers and 5–6 whole fresh basil leaves before popping it into the oven.

Shaping the Dough

- Remove the dough from the bowl and, on a floured surface, knead it for a couple minutes.

- Form it into a ball and cover it for 30–45 minutes. Once it has risen, divide it into two pieces.

- Form each piece into a ball and let sit for 20 minutes. (Use both pieces to make 2 pizzas or just one, refrigerating the other.)

- To form the pizza, stretch out the dough by pulling at the edges until it forms a circle that is flat at the center and raised at the sides.

Ricotta Spread

- In a saucepan over medium-high heat, heat up oil, and add onion and garlic. Sauté until onions are soft, then add milk, wine, and herbs.

- Reduce heat; allow sauce to simmer 5–10 minutes, until reduced and thickened. Remove sauce from heat and cool.

PASTA WITH PESTO & PEAS
Making your own pesto is easy and satisfying

If you have a blender, you can make pesto. For this recipe, you can always buy store-bought pesto, but whipping up your own version at home is so easy and satisfying, and will be fresher than anything sold in a jar.

Pesto can be made in different ways. Most commonly, it is made with basil, olive oil, garlic, and pine nuts, ground together. Basil is a fragrant and peppery herb often used in Italian cooking. A relative of peppermint, it can quite easily be grown at home in a garden or on a windowsill. Basil boasts several important health benefits, including antibacterial and anti-inflammatory properties. When added to foods, it acts as a natural preservative.

Yield: 1

KNACK CALORIE COUNTER COOKBOOK

Ingredients

2 ounces dried linguine

4 tablespoons pine nuts, divided

3 tablespoons olive oil

$1/4$ cup finely chopped fresh basil

1 clove garlic

Sea salt and freshly ground pepper, to taste

$1/4$ cup fresh or frozen peas

Calories ~750, **Fat** (g) 78, **Carbohydrates** (g) 54, **Protein** (g) 14, **Fiber** (g) 5, **Saturated Fat** (g) 9, **Cholesterol** (mg) 0, **Sodium** (mg) 473

Pasta with Pesto & Peas

- Bring a pot of salted water to a boil, then add the pasta and reduce heat.

- Let pasta simmer until it's al dente. Toast pine nuts, then set aside 1 tablespoon, using the rest for pesto.

- Make pesto with oil, basil, garlic, nuts, salt and pepper.

- Toss the peas in with the pasta for the last 2–3 minutes of cooking.

- Drain and toss with pesto.

Parsley or Cilantro Pesto: Instead of using basil, substitute ¼ cup fresh parsley or fresh cilantro. This will slightly change the taste of the pesto, and will infuse your pesto with slightly different health benefits. (Cilantro is great for digestive disorders.)

Cashew Pesto: You can also replace the pine nuts in this recipe with cashews, which impart a slightly nuttier flavor, and happen to have a lower fat content than other nuts. Prepare the pesto as described below, expect substitute the pine nuts for ¼ cup raw unsalted cashews.

Making Pesto

Tossing Pasta with Peas

- Place the pine nuts in a baking dish. Spray them with olive oil and, in an oven heated to 350°F, toast them for 5–10 minutes.

- Once they're lightly toasted, set aside 1 tablespoon; use the rest for the pesto.

- To make pesto, combine the olive oil, fresh basil, garlic, 3 tablespoons of toasted pine nuts, and salt and pepper in a blender or food processor and blend until smooth.

- Before draining the pasta, toss in the peas for 2–3 minutes.

- Drain the pasta and peas in a colander over a sink.

- Toss the pesto with the pasta, and top with the extra pine nuts.

QUICK DINNER

CHICKEN STROGANOFF

This Russian classic gets a makeover with lean chicken breast

Stroganoff is one of those soul-warming dishes that can't help but remind of you of a simpler time. This classic Russian dish became popular in the United States in the 1950s.

For this recipe, we've substituted lean chicken for the traditional beef. Some recipes call for the meat to be cubed, but here we've used chicken breast sliced into ½-inch-thick pieces. Slicing the breast on a diagonal will achieve the best aesthetic.

We've cut the fat and calories with our version of this dish by replacing the traditional sour cream with Greek-style non-fat plain yogurt. It's just as creamy and tangy as the original! *Yield: 1*

Ingredients

2 ounces dried egg noodles

1 tablespoon olive oil

½ onion, diced

1 clove garlic, minced

Sea salt and freshly ground pepper

4 ounces chicken breast, sliced into ½-inch-thick pieces

½ cup chopped fresh mushrooms

¼ cup canned tomatoes

3 tablespoons plain nonfat yogurt

Calories 706, **Fat** (g) 28, **Carbohydrates** (g) 59, **Protein** (g) 53, **Fiber** (g) 4, **Saturated Fat** (g) 6, **Cholesterol** (mg) 123, **Sodium** (mg) 309

Chicken Stroganoff

- Cook pasta in boiling salted water. Drain and rinse under cold water.

- In a skillet over medium-high heat, heat oil; add onions and garlic. Sauté until onions are soft, then remove and set aside.

- Season chicken. Spray pan with a bit more olive oil, and add chicken. Sauté until nearly done, then return onions and garlic to skillet; add mushrooms.

- Pour tomatoes into skillet, then stir in yogurt. Let stroganoff simmer for 10 minutes. Serve over noodles.

172

Beef Stroganoff: We use chicken, but there's nothing wrong with using the traditional beef for this dish. Many cuts of beef can be just as lean as chicken. Look for cuts that contain the word "loin" or "round" in the name, as these tend to be the leanest. If you use beef, you can cube it, as certain recipes call for, or slice it, as we've done with the chicken.

Ground Stroganoff: We've also seen stroganoff recipes that call for ground meat. In this case, you should use lean ground beef. Alternatively, you can look for lean ground turkey. Season the meat and brown it in a skillet before adding the rest of the ingredients, as is described below.

Slicing the Chicken

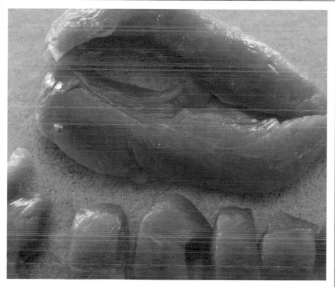

- Start with a clean breast of chicken. Rinse it under cold water, then pat it dry.

- On a cutting board, using a sharp chef's knife, hold the chicken with one hand and angle your knife on a slant with the other.

- Slice down on an angle into breast in smooth, clean strokes.

Sautéing the Chicken

- To sauté the chicken, make sure the skillet or pan is hot.

- Heat up no more than a tablespoon of oil and be sure not to let it smoke.

- Add the chicken pieces and, using a wooden spoon, stir them occasionally so that they cook evenly.

- Remove the chicken to cook vegetables and mushrooms, as these contain water and can prevent your meat from browning properly.

QUICK DINNER

173

STUFFED PEPPERS

This easy recipe makes for a colorful and delicious meal

Stuffed peppers are not only a healthy, tasty meal, but also a pretty picture. Use a combination of red, yellow, orange, and green bell peppers to make your dish as colorful as possible.

Bell peppers are an excellent source of vitamin C and vitamin A, two antioxidants that help fight the free radicals that can lead to cholesterol buildup in the arteries. In addition, they contain beta-carotene, which, among other things, can help prevent cataracts.

Different peppers also impart different flavors. Green peppers are unripe bell peppers and so have a slightly more bitter taste. Red, yellow, and orange peppers are sweeter.
Yield: 2

KNACK CALORIE COUNTER COOKBOOK

Ingredients

¹/₄ pound fresh turkey sausage

1 tablespoon olive oil

2 cloves garlic, minced

¹/₂ cup chopped mushrooms

³/₄ cup cooked rice

¹/₂ teaspoon turmeric

¹/₄ cup finely chopped fresh parsley

Sea salt and freshly ground pepper, to taste

2 bell peppers, tops cut off and seeded

Calories 214, **Fat** (g) 6, **Carbohydrates** (g) 30, **Protein** (g) 12, **Fiber** (g) 4, **Saturated Fat** (g) 2, **Cholesterol** (mg) 30, **Sodium** (mg) 526

Stuffed Peppers

- Slice open sausages and remove meat from the casings. In a skillet over medium-high heat, heat oil and toss in garlic. Add sausage and brown.

- Remove meat from skillet; add mushrooms. Cook a few minutes, until soft, then return meat to skillet, stirring well.

- Combine cooked rice with meat mixture. Add turmeric, parsley, and salt and pepper.

- Add mixture to peppers. Bake in a 375°F preheated oven 25–30 minutes.

Cutting off Tops of Peppers

Adding Mixture & Prepping for Oven

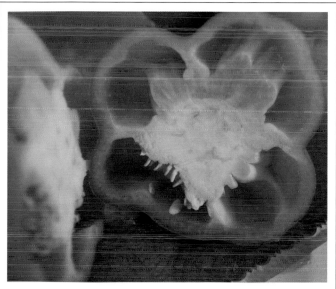

- Using a sharp chef's knife, slice the tops off the bell peppers.

- Using a smaller paring knife, seed the peppers by removing the membranes and seeds.

- The peppers should be entirely hollow for stuffing.

- Spoon half the mixture into each pepper.

- Place the peppers in a baking dish so that they stand up and don't topple over while baking.

- Once cooked, removed from oven, and cooled, use tongs to gently place stuffed peppers onto serving dish.

BAKED MEATBALLS IN MARINARA

These meatballs are not quite like Mom's—they're better (for you)!

This classic Italian dish is actually much lighter than it sounds. When shopping for your ingredients, look for lean ground turkey meat for the meatballs.

This recipe calls for San Marzano canned tomatoes, a variety of plum tomato that grows at the base of Mount Vesuvius, near Naples in Italy. They are said to make the best tomato sauces because of the rich volcanic soil in which they grow. If you cannot find this type, use any canned plum tomatoes.

Unlike many canned foods, canned tomatoes retain most of their nutrients. They are also high in potassium while being low in sodium, which can help lower blood pressure.

Yield: 6 servings

Ingredients

1 tablespoon olive oil

1 yellow onion, diced

5 cloves garlic, minced, divided

1/2 cup red or white wine

1 28-ounce can San Marzano tomatoes

5 ounces tomato paste

1/2 cup chopped fresh cilantro

1 teaspoon dried oregano

1 teaspoon dried basil

Sea salt and freshly ground pepper, to taste

1 pound ground turkey breast

1/4 cup whole wheat bread crumbs

2 egg whites

Calories 212, **Fat** (g) 9, **Carbohydrates** (g) 15, **Protein** (g) 17, **Fiber** (g) 2, **Saturated Fat** (g) 3, **Cholesterol** (mg) 61, **Sodium** (mg) 477

Baked Meatballs in Marinara

- In a large pot over medium heat, heat oil. Add onion and 3 minced garlic cloves. Sauté until onions are soft.

- Add wine and simmer 10–12 minutes, until liquid is reduced. Add tomatoes, tomato paste, herbs, and salt and pepper. Allow it to simmer for half an hour.

- In a mixing bowl, combine turkey, bread crumbs, remaining garlic, egg whites, and salt and pepper.

- Shape and bake meatballs. Transfer them to sauce.

· · · · RECIPE VARIATION · · · ·

Angel Hair & Meatballs: For a gentle twist on spaghetti and meatballs, cook 12 ounces dried angel hair pasta until al dente. Remember, these delicate noodles don't take more than 5 minutes to cook. Serve 2–3 meatballs, in their sauce, atop 1 cup cooked pasta.

Sauce Simmering

- After adding wine to the sauce, allow it to simmer for 10–12 minutes, which will allow for the liquid to reduce.

- After adding the next round of ingredients, the sauce will have to simmer for 15 minutes.

Forming and Baking Meatballs

- Mix the meatball ingredients well with your hands, then shape the meat into golf-ball-size pieces.

- Spray a baking dish with olive oil and place the meatballs in the dish. In an oven preheated to 350°F, bake the meatballs for 20–25 minutes.

- Remove the meatballs from the oven and place them on a paper towel to soak up any excess grease.

KOREAN BIBIMBAP

Make this East Asian favorite the next time you want to try something new

This simple dish is found everywhere in South Korea. Incorporating rice, cut vegetables, and an egg on top, it is a great source of vitamins, minerals, fiber, and protein. This recipe calls for brown rice, as well as a selection of snappy vegetables, sliced thin.

The original is served very hot in a clay pot and a raw egg is cracked over the top. Because the pot and rice are so hot, the egg cooks right there in the bowl. For this version, we use a fried egg, which is laid on top of the bibimbap before serving.

Yield: 2 servings

KNACK CALORIE COUNTER COOKBOOK

Ingredients

1 tablespoon sesame oil

2 tablespoons soy sauce

1 teaspoon hoisin sauce

1 clove garlic, minced

1 cup sliced shiitake mushrooms

1 cup julienned carrots

1 zucchini, sliced

2 eggs

1 cup cooked brown rice

1 cup baby spinach

1 cup bean sprouts

Sriracha, to taste

Calories 325, **Fat** (g) 13, **Carbohydrates** (g) 44, **Protein** (g) 12, **Fiber** (g) 7, **Saturated Fat** (g) 3, **Cholesterol** (mg) 186, **Sodium** (mg) 134

Korean Bibimbap

- In a skillet over medium-high, heat up the oil, soy sauce, and hoisin sauce. Toss in the garlic and mushrooms. Sauté. Remove.

- Add carrots. Cook until soft, then remove; add zucchini. Cook until soft, then remove.

- Crack egg into skillet. Cook sunny-side up.

- Spoon cooked rice into a bowl and arrange veggies around it, including raw baby spinach and sprouts.

- Place egg on top. The heat from the rice and egg should steam spinach slightly.

••••• RECIPE VARIATIONS •••••

Beefy Bibimbap: The dish can also be served with ground beef. In a skillet over medium heat, cook ¼ pound of lean ground beef, until browned. Allow it to cool a little before adding it to the bibimbap.

Spicy Bibimbap: Kick up the spice in your bibimbap by flavoring the dish with Sriracha, a popular Asian condiment made with chiles and garlic. The dish is normally served with the ingredients separate in the bowl. Add a squirt of Sriracha and use chopsticks to toss everything together. But be careful—it's spicy!

Sautéing Mushrooms

- Mushrooms are mostly water and so will shrink as you cook them.

- Depending on your preference, you may want them to simply soften a little or you may prefer them to brown.

- Heat up your oil in the skillet, then add the mushrooms. Stir them as they cook. Be careful not to overcook—they shouldn't take more than a few minutes.

Making Brown Rice

- For perfect rice, heat 1 teaspoon of olive oil in a saucepan over medium-high heat.

- Dump 1 cup of rice into the saucepan, and sauté the rice for a minute or so.

- Pour 2½ cups of salted water over the rice, and bring it to a boil. (The amount of water is based on the type of rice—the more robust the grain, the more water needed.)

- Allow the rice to simmer in a covered pot over very low heat for 20 minutes, or until it's cooked through. Drain if necessary.

BAKED VEGETABLE LASAGNA
There are few dishes more comforting than baked lasagna

Baked lasagna is one of those dishes that is delicious when it's right out of the oven and the cheese on top is still bubbling but is even better the next day. Or the day after. This recipe calls for zucchini, mushrooms, carrots, celery, and onions, but you can toss in any vegetables you like.

You can also up the density, as well as the protein content of your lasagna by adding meat to your tomato sauce. Use lean ground beef, such as ground sirloin or round.

Of course, the fun of making a lasagna is layering the pasta, sauce and cheese. Use a smaller baking dish for more layers—but you should aim for at least three or four.
Yield: 6–8 servings

Baked Vegetable Lasagna

Ingredients

1 tablespoon olive oil

1 onion, diced

4 cloves garlic, minced

2 stalks celery, chopped

3 carrots, sliced

1 cup chopped fresh mushrooms

1/2 cup chopped fresh cilantro

1 teaspoon dried oregano

1 teaspoon dried basil

1/2 cup red or white wine

1 28-ounce can San Marzano tomatoes

5 ounces tomato paste

Sea salt and freshly ground pepper, to taste

1 egg white

1 cup low-fat ricotta

1 cup low-fat cottage cheese

1 box dried whole wheat lasagna noodles

4 zucchini, sliced

1 cup shredded mozzarella

Calories 383, **Fat** (g) 9, **Carbohydrates** (g) 59, **Protein** (g) 23, **Fiber** (g) 8, **Saturated Fat** (g) 4, **Cholesterol** (mg) 18, **Sodium** (mg) 619

KNACK CALORIE COUNTER COOKBOOK

- In a large pot over medium heat, heat oil; add onion and garlic. Sauté until onions are soft. Add celery, carrots, mushrooms, and herbs.

- Add wine; simmer 10–12 minutes, until liquid is reduced. Stir in canned tomatoes and paste. Season

- sauce; simmer on low heat half an hour.

- Make mixture from egg white, ricotta, and cottage cheese; cook pasta. Layer lasagna. Sprinkle with mozzarella.

- In a 250°F preheated oven, bake lasagna 45 minutes.

• • • • RECIPE VARIATIONS • • • •

Spinach Lasagna: Add fresh or frozen spinach to the dish by layering the spinach in with the pasta, sauce, and cheese. Sauté the spinach for a few minutes beforehand. If using frozen spinach, you may need to add a few drops of water to it to reconstitute it.

Meat Lasagna: Turn this into a meat lasagna with a little lean ground beef or lean ground turkey. In a skillet over medium-high heat, sauté 1 pound of lean ground meat with some salt and pepper and a minced clove of garlic. Once the meat is almost well done, add it to the simmering sauce.

Mixing Ingredients and Cooking Pasta

- In a mixing bowl, combine egg white, ricotta, and cottage cheese.

- Add noodles to a pot of boiling, salted water; cook until al dente.

Layering Lasagna

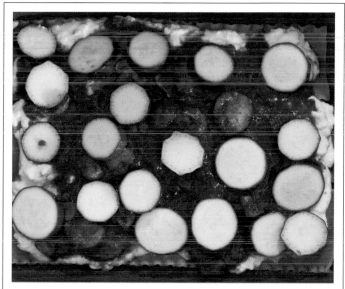

- In a rectangular glass dish sprayed with olive oil, layer the noodles, cheese mixture, sauce, and zucchini.

- Repeat these layers until you've used all the ingredients.

- Depending on the size of your dish, you'll end up with three or four layers. Sprinkle the top layer with mozzarella.

MARINATED BEEF KEBABS
Make these colorful kebabs in an oven indoors or on a grill outside

Shish kebabs are associated with summer barbecues, but they can easily be made indoors in an oven. Because the ingredients are all cut into bite-size pieces, they cook up pretty quickly. So be careful not to overdo the kebabs, regardless of where you cook them.

We've made this recipe with beef cubes, bell peppers, and white button mushrooms, but you can choose to skewer any number of meats and veggies for your kebabs.

You can use metal or wood skewers for your kebabs, but keep in mind that metal heats up quickly and takes a long time to cool down. So, handle with care. On the other hand, they're far more environmentally friendly than disposable wood.

Yield: 1

Ingredients

¹/₄ pound lean beef, cubed

Sea salt and freshly ground pepper, to taste

¹/₂ red bell pepper, cubed

¹/₂ yellow bell pepper, cubed

1 cup fresh button mushrooms, halved

¹/₄ cup marinade (recipe follows)

For the marinade:

¹/₄ cup olive oil

2 tablespoons Worcestershire sauce

1 teaspoon French mustard

1 clove garlic, minced

Calories 483, **Fat** (g) 40, **Carbohydrates** (g) 16, **Protein** (g) 19, **Fiber** (g) 3, **Saturated Fat** (g) 11, **Cholesterol** (mg) 58, **Sodium** (mg) 715

Marinated Beef Kebabs

- In a bowl, combine the olive oil, Worcestershire sauce, mustard, and garlic. Whisk together well.

- Marinate beef cubes for at least 20 minutes. Salt and pepper meat. Assemble kabobs with peppers, meat, and mushrooms.

- On a grill, cook kebabs 5–8 minutes on each side.

- If you don't have a grill, you can make these in the oven. Place kebabs in a baking dish and, in a 375°F pre-heated oven, cook 15–18 minutes, turning once.

• • • • RECIPE VARIATIONS • • • •

Veggie Kebabs: Add cherry tomatoes, roughly chopped red onion, and sliced zucchini (not too thin—say, ¼-inch thick) to your kebabs, several of each per skewer. Intersperse these with your marinated beef cubes for a varied and colorful kebab.

Chicken Kebabs: Instead of using beef, skewer cubes of chicken. If you're using an oven instead of a grill, you'll want to sear these in a skillet for a minute or so on all sides before popping them in the oven.

Making Up Skewers

- Salt and pepper the meat.

- Skewer the bell peppers, meat cubes, and mushrooms on a stick, making each kebab as colorful and diverse as possible.

- If using wood, be careful not to get splinters in the meat, by rubbing two skewers against each other before threading to smooth them out.

Marinating Kebabs

- You can marinate the kebab meat in a shallow dish, or you can place it in a large, tightly sealed food storage bag.

- The latter can offer better overall coating of the meat.

- Marinate the meat for at least 20 minutes, turning once if in a dish, before threading onto a skewer.

JAMBALAYA

This Creole favorite doesn't have to be a heavy meal

Jambalaya is a Louisiana staple. Loosely related to Spanish paella, it is usually made with a mixture of rice, chicken, seafood, and sausage, such as a hearty and spicy andouille sausage.

This version of the dish is lighter than a traditional jambalaya. Using brown rice, chicken breast, and turkey sausage, we've managed to reduce the calorie value of the original dish while boosting its nutritional value. Traditionally, jambalaya also calls for shrimp. You can add jumbo shrimp to this dish, upping the protein and iron in it.

Yield: 2 servings

Ingredients

2 tablespoons olive oil, divided

1 stalk celery, chopped

1 shallot, chopped

1 boneless skinless chicken breast, cubed

1 cooked spicy turkey sausage, cubed

2 cloves garlic, minced

1 cup brown rice

1 1/2 cups chicken stock

1 ounce tomato paste

Pinch of cayenne pepper

Pinch of cumin

Sea salt and freshly ground pepper, to taste

1 bay leaf

1/4 cup chopped fresh parsley

Calories 700, **Fat** (g) 35, **Carbohydrates** (g) 36, **Protein** (g) 59, **Fiber** (g) 4, **Saturated Fat** (g) 5, **Cholesterol** (mg) 129, **Sodium** (mg) 1406

Jambalaya

- In a skillet over medium-high heat, heat half of oil; add celery and shallots.

- Sauté until soft, then remove. Sauté chicken until browned, then return celery and shallots to skillet. Add sausage.

- Make the rice. When rice is almost done, give it a stir, then add in chicken mixture. Stir in paste, cayenne, cumin, bay leaf, and salt and pepper. Stir in parsley at the end. Keep covered until rice is tender.

• • • • RECIPE VARIATIONS • • • •

Shrimp Jambalaya: Sauté deveined jumbo shrimp over medium-high heat until they start to turn pink. Remove them from heat before they're cooked through, then add them to the rice at the same time as the chicken and sausage. Let the shrimp finish cooking in the pot.

Smoky Jambalaya: To change the flavors in your jambalaya, smoke it! Prepare the dish as described below, except replace your cooked turkey sausage with a smoked sausage. The smoky flavors will be imparted to the rest of your dish.

Chicken Sautéing

- To sauté the chicken, make sure the skillet is already hot.

- Heat up your oil but be sure not to let it start to smoke.

- Toss in the chicken and let the individual pieces brown on one side before stirring or turning them to brown the other side.

Make the Rice

- In a large pot over high heat, heat the rest of the oil and toss in garlic and rice.

- Sauté rice for a few minutes before adding stock. You may need to top it up with water to make sure it's well covered. Bring stock to a boil, then reduce heat to low. Cook covered 15–20 minutes, until rice is done.

FAST FRUITY FROZEN YOGURT

This makeshift fruity frozen yogurt is a sweet and refreshing snack

It's not quite ice cream but it can be just as rewarding, especially on a warm evening. Frozen yogurt is a great way to fulfill that craving you have for something cold and sweet. And you don't need an ice cream maker to make this delicious frozen yogurt. Using frozen berries, plain nonfat yogurt, and a touch of honey, you create a frozen snack that will refresh you while satisfying those after-dinner cravings.

We've suggested blending fresh fruits into your frozen yogurt. You can also use fresh fruit or nuts as toppings for your snack. And there's no better way to garnish a refreshing bowl of frozen yogurt than with a fresh sprig of mint—it looks pretty, too!

Yield: 1

Ingredients

¹/₂ cup plain nonfat yogurt

Handful of frozen raspberries

¹/₂ teaspoon vanilla extract

1 tablespoon honey

Fast Fruity Frozen Yogurt

- Combine all the ingredients in a blender, and blend until smooth.

- The riper the fruit, the sweeter the frozen yogurt will be.

Calories 186, **Fat** (g) 2, **Carbohydrates** (g) 32, **Protein** (g) 7, **Fiber** (g) 2, **Saturated Fat** (g) 1, **Cholesterol** (mg) 7, **Sodium** (mg) 81

• • • • RECIPE VARIATIONS • • • •

Other Frozen Yogurts: We've made this fruity frozen yogurt with raspberries, but you can use any fruits, from blueberries, blackberries, and strawberries to peaches, bananas, and kiwis. To make a chocolaty frozen yogurt, use a frozen banana and a tablespoon of cocoa powder.

Vanilla Frozen Yogurt: To make the flavors really pop, use half a fresh vanilla bean. Simply slice open the bean lengthwise, and using a fine paring knife, scrape off all the inside seeds. Toss them into the blender with the other ingredients for intense vanilla flavor.

Blending Ingredients

- Blend the ingredients on high speed.

- Make sure the fruit is still frozen when you blend.

- Make sure the yogurt is cold so that it doesn't bring down the temperature of the frozen berries too much.

Freezing Berries

- Use fresh, clean, ripe berries.

- Spread the berries out on a cookie sheet and freeze them overnight.

- The next day, transfer them to a sealable storage bag or container.

- This way, the berries won't stick together.

- If you have more berries, repeat the first step and add them to the sealable container.

CHEX MIX

The original party mix still makes a great, light snack

Chex party mix is easy and fun to make for friends or just to store for yourself when you get a case of the munchies. You can season it any way you like using dried spices, then bake it until it's golden brown. The mix lasts for several weeks in an airtight sealed container . . . although it's unlikely to last too long, considering how tasty it is!

For this recipe, we've used your favorite crackers, commercial cereals and snacks, and tossed them with olive oil and an irresistible blend of flavors. But feel free to get creative with your seasonings. . . . After all, there are no rules when it comes to a party mix.

Yield: 8

Ingredients

1 cup Corn Chex

1 cup Rice Chex

1 cup Multi-Bran Chex

1 cup plain Cheerios

¹/₂ cup plain Goldfish Crackers

¹/₂ cup unsalted peanuts

¹/₂ cup pretzel sticks

¹/₄ cup olive oil

2 teaspoons Worcestershire sauce

¹/₂ teaspoon celery salt

¹/₂ teaspoon paprika

¹/₂ teaspoon cayenne pepper

¹/₂ teaspoon garlic powder

¹/₄ teaspoon ground ginger

Calories 222, **Fat** (g) 16, **Carbohydrates** (g) 19, **Protein** (g) 4, **Fiber** (g) 3, **Saturated Fat** (g) 2, **Cholesterol** (mg) 0, **Sodium** (mg) 210

Chex Mix

- In a large mixing bowl, toss together all the ingredients.

- Spread the mixture out on a cookie sheet and, in an oven preheated to 350°F, bake for 25–30 minutes, turning every 10 minutes or so.

- Allow the mix to cool before serving or storing.

Asian Chex Mix: Spice up your Chex mix Asian-style in a few easy steps. Swap out the peanuts for wasabi peanuts, and swap out the pretzel sticks for dried chow mein noodles. Instead of Worcestershire sauce, toss the Chex with soy sauce. Alternatively, mix up the soy sauce with a tablespoon of Sriracha, and toss your dry mixture with that. The other spices can stay the same.

Spicy Chex Mix: Prepare the snack as is described below, except add an extra ½ teaspoon of chili powder to the mixture. You can also kick this up by tossing it with a few dashes of your favorite hot sauce to make it as spicy as you like!

Tossing Ingredients Together

- You may want to create an emulsion of the olive oil and the Worcestershire sauce to facilitate coating all the ingredients.

- Use your hands to toss the ingredients to avoid breaking any of the delicate Chex squares!

Turning the Chex Mix

- Use a spatula or wooden spoon to turn and shuffle the different ingredients as they bake.

- This will allow them to cook evenly.

INDOOR S'MORES

You don't need a campfire to enjoy this classic snack

Relive your favorite camping experiences from the comfort of your own home with this quick and easy s'mores recipe.

All you need are the building blocks of s'mores: chocolate, graham crackers, and marshmallow. The calorie content of this snack is actually quite low, especially if you use bittersweet chocolate chips, which contain less fat and calories than milk chocolate.

Layering your s'mores is half the fun—the other half being eating them of course! This is the kind of snack that's fun to make with friends. But don't be shy about treating yourself to it—it's the perfect light-hearted midnight snack.

Yield: 1

Ingredients

1 whole graham cracker, broken in half

1 marshmallow

1 teaspoon mini bittersweet chocolate chips

Calories 116, **Fat** (g) 4, **Carbohydrates** (g) 21, **Protein** (g) 1, **Fiber** (g) 1, **Saturated Fat** (g) 1, **Cholesterol** (mg) 1, **Sodium** (mg) 91

Indoor S'mores

- Place half the graham cracker on a cookie sheet and layer with the chocolate chips and marshmallow.

- Place the other half of the cracker next to it on the cookie sheet.

- In an oven preheated to 400°F, bake the open s'more for 5–8 minutes, or until the chocolate is melting.

- Allow the s'more to cool a little before putting on the top and serving.

Make Your Own Marshmallows: Soften 3 ounces of unflavored gelatin in 1 cup of hot water over a double boiler. Dissolve 3 cups of superfine sugar into 2 cups of hot water. Pour the gelatin mixture and sugar mixture into the bowl of an electric mixer and immediately start whipping them together on high speed. Once the mixture becomes fluffy, spoon it out into a lightly oiled bak-ing dish sprinkled with powdered sugar. Let the mixture set uncovered overnight. Turn the marshmallows out onto a clean surface and slice into cubes.

Coconutty S'Mores: Sprinkle ½ teaspoon of coconut shavings onto the chocolate chips on the graham cracker before adding the marshmallow and toasting.

How Many Calories?

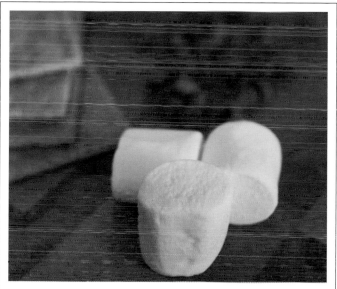

- A plain or honey graham cracker is just 60 calories per large rectangular cracker.

- A regular-sized marshmallow is just 23 calories.

- A teaspoon of bittersweet chocolate chips is just 23 calories.

Layering S'mores

- To layer your s'more, start with the graham cracker square (half a large rectangular graham cracker).

- Pile on the chocolate chips, making sure none slip off the edge.

- Balance the marshmallow on end on top.

- Close the s'more after it's been toasted by carefully pressing down with the top layer to smoosh it together.

MAPLE POPCORN

Who needs a snack in a box when you can make your own sweet popcorn?

Pure maple syrup makes this snack a sweet treat. Use an air popper to make the popcorn, if you have one, or pop it in a pot on the stovetop. We like to think this snack is even more satisfying than store-bought versions of it because you can enjoy it warm and sticky straight from the pot.

Maple syrup is not only packed with manganese and zinc, but sweet enough that you don't have to use tons of it. And you can always swap out the maple syrup for iron-rich blackstrap molasses. Add peanuts to the mix for an extra satisfying crunch.

Yield: 1

Ingredients

1 tablespoon butter

1 tablespoon grade A or B maple syrup

1/4 teaspoon vanilla extract

Pinch of salt

2 cups air-popped popcorn

Calories 219, **Fat** (g) 12, **Carbohydrates** (g) 26, **Protein** (g) 2, **Fiber** (g) 2, **Saturated Fat** (g) 7, **Cholesterol** (mg) 31, **Sodium** (mg) 395

Maple Popcorn

- In a saucepan over low heat, melt the butter and stir in the maple syrup, vanilla extract, and salt.

- Remove the sauce from the heat and toss with the popcorn, coating each kernel well.

- Spread out the popcorn on a parchment-lined cookie sheet and, in an oven preheated to 325°F, bake the popcorn for 8–10 minutes.

- Allow the popcorn to cool a little before serving.

Crunchy Popcorn: Add an extra crunch to this snack by tossing a handful of unsalted peanuts into the mix. First toss the peanuts with the popcorn, then toss everything with the syrup for a makeshift Cracker Jack snack.

Molasses Popcorn: Instead of maple syrup, try using a good blackstrap molasses for this snack. Blackstrap molasses is loaded with iron for energy and calcium for bone and muscle health. It also contains significant amounts of magnesium, copper, potassium, and manganese, all essential nutrients for a healthy body. Best of all, blackstrap molasses is fat free.

Melting the Butter

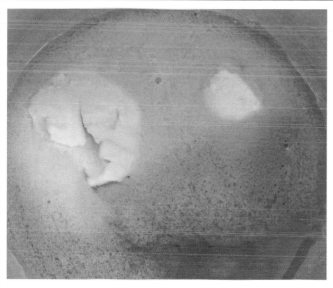

- To melt the butter without burning it, heat it over low heat, stirring constantly.
- Stir in the other ingredients to ensure everything is well mixed.

Spreading the Popcorn

- Spread the popcorn mixture out on a baking sheet using a spatula or wooden spoon.
- To avoid having the mixture stick to your utensil, try spraying it lightly with vegetable oil.

CHOCOLATE-COVERED PRETZELS
Melted semisweet chocolate turns regular pretzels into a salty-sweet snack

When we have the munchies, some of us crave sweet and some of us crave salty. Satisfy everyone's cravings with these salty-sweet chocolate-covered pretzels.

For this snack, you can use thin, finger-long pretzel sticks or bite-size knot-shaped pretzels. If you find other fun pretzel shapes, such as pretzel twists or pretzel Goldfish, feel free to use them to make this snack.

Yield: 1

Ingredients

¹/₂ cup bittersweet chocolate chips

1 cup pretzel sticks

Calories 510, **Fat** (g) 26, **Carbohydrates** (g) 75, **Protein** (g) 6, **Fiber** (g) 6, **Saturated Fat** (g) 15, **Cholesterol** (mg) 0, **Sodium** (mg) 91

Chocolate-covered Pretzels

- In a saucepan or double boiler over low heat, melt the chocolate chips, stirring constantly.

- Dip each pretzel stick three-quarters of the way into the chocolate. If you're using knot-shaped pretzels, dip them halfway.

- Lay out the pretzels on a piece of waxed paper.

- Refrigerate the pretzels uncovered for an hour, then serve.

Nutty Chocolate-covered Pretzels: Add a satisfying crunch to this snack with some chopped nuts, which will also up the protein content. Finely chop a handful of peanuts, either by hand with a sharp chef's knife or by tossing them in a food processor and pressing the pulse button for a few seconds. Place the chopped nuts in a shallow bowl or plate. Immediately after dipping each pretzel in chocolate, roll it in the chopped nuts until coated.

Crispy Chocolate-covered Pretzels: Prepare your snack as described below, except take 2 tablespoons of Rice Krispies cereal and crush them lightly. Sprinkle the crushed cereal onto the freshly dipped pretzels, then lay them out on the wax paper.

Melting Chocolate

- To melt your chocolate evenly without burning it, stir it constantly over low heat.

- You can also use a double boiler, which consists of two fitted saucepans that fit one over the other.

- The bottom one contains water that is brought to a boil.

- The chocolate goes in the top saucepan, which will melt over the heat of the bottom one.

Dipping Pretzels

- To avoid burning your fingers on the hot chocolate, use a pair of tongs to hold each pretzel as you dip it.

- When the pretzel comes out of the chocolate, gently shake off the excess chocolate.

- Wait until the pretzel stops dripping before laying it out to harden.

CHAI TEA

Brew up this flavorful Indian-style tea as a hot, drinkable snack

In India, *chai* simply means "tea." But to Westerners, the term has come to refer to what Indians call *masala chai,* a delicious mixture of hot black tea with milk and various aromatic Indian spices. The recipe can change quite drastically from one part of India to another, but most versions contain some combination of cardamom, cinnamon, peppercorns, and cloves. They can also include star anise and ginger.

Make this tea with green tea instead of black for an extra antioxidant boost. You can also boost the protein content in this hot drink by making it with soy milk instead of skim milk.

Yield: 1

Ingredients

3 green cardamom pods

6 whole dried cloves

1 cinnamon stick

3 whole black peppercorns

3 cups water

1 tablespoon Darjeeling tea leaves

4 ounces nonfat milk

1 1/2 tablespoons honey

Calories 207, **Fat** (g) 3, **Carbohydrates** (g) 45, **Protein** (g) 6, **Fiber** (g) 6, **Saturated Fat** (g) 1, **Cholesterol** (mg) 2, **Sodium** (mg) 96

Chai Tea

- In a saucepan, combine the cardamom, cloves, cinnamon stick, peppercorns, and water. Bring to a boil over high heat.

- Remove the mixture from the heat and steep for 10 minutes. Then add the loose tea and bring to a boil once again.

- Reduce the heat and let the tea simmer for 5 minutes.

- Strain the tea and return the liquid to the saucepan. Stir in the milk and honey, and serve.

Green Chai Tea: Try brewing this tea using green tea instead of black. And instead of peppercorns, use the subtle, precious spice saffron, if you can find it. Bring the spices to a boil, then remove them from the heat. Let steep for 10 minutes. Add loose green tea and boil again, then let simmer and drain.

Soy Chai Tea: Make this hot drink as described below, except instead of using skim milk, add 4 ounces of unflavored and unsweetened soy milk to the tea. You can save the steeped tea in a sealed container in the fridge, then warm it up when you're ready to add the milk.

Steeping Spices

- Allow the spices to steep for 10 minutes or so off the heat.

- You can use this spice mixture as a homemade base for instant chai.

- Let it cool, then store in a sealed plastic container in the fridge until you're ready to use it.

Stirring in Milk

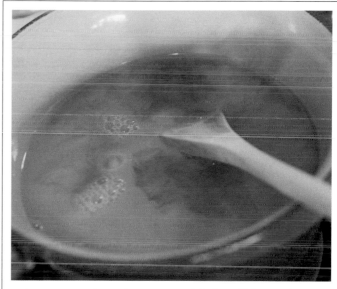

- Be sure not to burn the milk.

- Stir the milk in over low heat, and keep it over the heat just long enough to warm the tea, maybe 5–8 minutes.

HERBED POPCORN
Movie-style has nothing on this sophisticated popcorn snack

If you thought butter and salt were the only way to enjoy a bowl of popcorn, think again. Subtle herbs and spices and grated Parmesan cheese add color and flavor to air-popped or plain stovetop popcorn.

If you don't have an air-popper, popping corn on the stovetop is easy and imparts a nice toasted taste to the corn. If popping your corn on the stovetop, you'll need to add a bit of oil to the recipe (increasing the caloric value of the snack).

Use any type of vegetable oil, but make sure not to let it get hot enough that it starts to smoke.
Yield: 2 cups

Ingredients

2 cups air-popped popcorn

2 teaspoons finely grated Parmesan cheese

$1/2$ teaspoon garlic powder

$1/2$ teaspoon dried oregano

$1/2$ teaspoon dried thyme

$1/4$ teaspoon cayenne pepper

Sea salt, to taste

Herbed Popcorn

- Spray your freshly popped corn with a mist of olive oil.

- Immediately (while it's still hot) toss the lightly oiled popcorn with the cheese and seasonings.

Calories 84, **Fat** (g) 2, **Carbohydrates** (g) 14, **Protein** (g) 4, **Fiber** (g) 3, **Saturated Fat** (g) 1, **Cholesterol** (mg) 3, **Sodium** (mg) 518

Stovetop Popcorn: Over medium-high, heat 2 teaspoons of oil. Pour ½ cup of kernels into the saucepan and cover it with the lid. Lift the saucepan and move it back and forth vigorously to shake up the kernels inside. Leave it on the heat as the kernels begin to pop, shaking the saucepan regularly to disperse the heat evenly. When the popping slows to every few seconds, cut the heat.

Curry Popcorn: Spice up your popcorn by adding savory Indian flavors to it. Prepare the popcorn as described below, except substitute the seasonings listed with ½ teaspoon curry powder, ¼ teaspoon turmeric, and ¼ teaspoon cayenne pepper. Add sea salt, to taste.

Air-popping Popcorn

Tossing Popcorn with Seasonings

- Make sure your popcorn is fresh, as stale popcorn doesn't pop.

- Remove the top of the machine and pour ½ cup of kernels into the popping chamber.

- Put the top back on and place a large bowl under the chute where the popcorn comes out.

- Turn the popper on and wait for the corn to start popping. Turn it off as the popping slows to every few seconds to avoid burning any kernels.

- Use your hands to toss the ingredients so that you can avoid breaking the delicate popped kernels.

MIXED OLIVES

This simple snack is packed with nutrients and health-promoting good fats

Olives are a fruit that tastes dreadfully bitter fresh and deliciously savory when cured. They come in a variety of colors and flavors, from tangy green to salty black. You buy olives already pitted or with the pit intact. Olives come stuffed with everything from pimientos to blanched almonds. They make an easy snack as they require little prep work, and can be stored for up to a year if they came in a jar. Loose olives stored in plastic should be consumed within a few weeks.

Not only a great source of monounsaturated fats, which are the best kind of fats, olives are also high in vitamin E.

Yield: 1

Ingredients

¹/₂ cup small green olives

¹/₂ cup queen olives

¹/₂ cup black olives

Juice of ¹/₂ lemon

¹/₂ teaspoon grated garlic

Pinch of sea salt

Mixed Olives

- In a bowl, combine the olives.

- Toss the olives with the lemon juice, garlic, and salt.

- Serve olives in a dish next to a smaller dish so that your guests have a place to put the pits.

Calories 180, **Fat** (g) 18, **Carbohydrates** (g) 4, **Protein** (g) 0,
Fiber (g) 0, **Saturated Fat** (g) 0, **Cholesterol** (mg) 0,
Sodium (mg) 2393

If there were ever a trend in olives, the most recent would be that of the Castelvetrano olive. This bright green, mild-flavored olive is picked young and cured in a lightly salted brine, which makes eating one like eating a fresh fruit. Castelvetranos add not only a buttery flavor, but also a shot of color to any olive dish.

Red Hot Chile Olives: Kick up your mixed olives with a little heat. Take 1 habanero pepper and slice it in half. Seed it and dice it. Toss ½ teaspoon of the pepper in with the other ingredients. You may wish to use gloves to handle the peppers to protect your skin and eyes (there's nothing worse than handling a hot pepper then scratching your eye!).

Grating Garlic

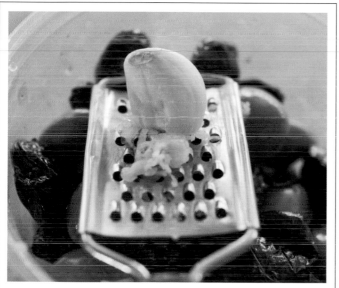

- Grating garlic is said to retain the garlic's sweetness more than pressing it. To grate garlic, use a cheese grater or lemon zester.

- Chop off the ends of the garlic using a sharp chef's knife.

- Using your palm, smack the side of the blade down onto the garlic to crack it slightly. This should make the garlic easier to peel.

- Gently run the garlic over the surface of the grater or zester at an angle.

Tossing Ingredients

- Use salad tongs or your hands to toss the olives with the other ingredients.

- Using your hands will minimize your chances of bruising or damaging the olives.

EVENING SNACKS TO GO

PEANUT BRITTLE

Make your own candy with this easy peanut brittle recipe

It may be a snack associated with county fairs and candy shops, but peanut brittle can make for a tasty salty-sweet snack that you don't have to feel too guilty about.

In this recipe, sugar and water combine to make a caramel to which unsalted peanuts are added. Cinnamon and vanilla add a depth of flavor to the brittle. Once the mixture has cooled, it's fun to take the butt of a knife to the solid brittle to break it up for a homemade candy snack.

Munch on it by itself for a snack or turn it into dessert by breaking it up over a bowl of low-fat vanilla ice cream or frozen yogurt.

Yield: 4

Ingredients

1 cup water

1 tablespoon unsalted butter

2 cups brown sugar

²/₃ cup honey

1 teaspoon vanilla extract

¹/₂ teaspoon cinnamon

Pinch of salt

1 cup raw peanuts

Calories 241, **Fat** (g) 9, **Carbohydrates** (g) 38, **Protein** (g) 5, **Fiber** (g) 2, **Saturated Fat** (g) 1, **Cholesterol** (mg) 0, **Sodium** (mg) 19

Peanut Brittle

- In a saucepan over high heat, combine the water, butter, honey, and sugar. Bring to a boil, stirring continuously.

- Reduce the heat, and cook until you have a dark brown caramel.

- Cut the heat and quickly stir in the vanilla extract, cinnamon, and salt, mixing well.

- Stir in the peanuts immediately. Layer on cookie sheet and press mixture, then refrigerate 1 hour. Remove the brittle from the fridge, break, and serve.

Maple Peanut Brittle: Add a touch of maple to this brittle by adding 2 tablespoons of maple syrup to the caramel mixture. Prepare it as below, except pour in the maple syrup once the sugar has dissolved in the saucepan.

Nutty Peanut Brittle: You may already know this, but peanuts are not in fact nuts. They're legumes. You can add nuts to this brittle for a, well, nuttier taste and crunchier texture. Prepare the caramel as described below, except when you add the peanuts, also toss ½ cup chopped hazelnuts into the mixture.

Stirring Peanuts into Caramel

Pressing Peanut Mixture into Cookie Sheet

- You want the caramel to still be warm while stirring in the ingredients.

- When stirring in the peanuts, be sure to do so immediately.

- As the mixture begins to cool, you'll have to use force.

- Once the peanuts are well coated, spread the mixture onto a waxed-paper-lined cookie sheet.

- When pressing peanut mixture onto the cookie sheet, press down on the mixture using another piece of waxed paper (so your hands don't stick).

- Later, remove the brittle from the fridge and break it into pieces using the butt of a knife.

ROASTED PUMPKIN SEEDS
Iron-rich pumpkin seeds are a savory snack you can take anywhere

Pumpkin seeds are packed with nutrients that are essential to both men and women. But men, especially, can get a lot out of snacking on pumpkin seeds. Studies have shown that the carotenoids—found not only in the flesh but also in the seeds of many orange foods, such as pumpkins—as well as the omega-3 fatty acids and zinc found in pumpkin seeds can help promote prostate health, as well as strong bones in men.

Pumpkin seeds make a great addition to any trail mix or even a tasty topping for a salad. We also like to nibble them just by themselves.

Yield: 1

Ingredients

¹/₂ cup whole raw pumpkin seeds

1 teaspoon olive oil

¹/₄ teaspoon cumin

¹/₄ teaspoon garlic powder

¹/₄ teaspoon cayenne pepper

Pinch of sea salt

Calories 185, **Fat** (g) 11, **Carbohydrates** (g) 18, **Protein** (g) 6, **Fiber** (g) 0, **Saturated Fat** (g) 2, **Cholesterol** (mg) 0, **Sodium** (mg) 84

Roasted Pumpkin Seeds

- In a bowl, combine the ingredients and toss well so that all the seeds are coated.

- Spread the seeds on a parchment-lined cookie sheet.

- In an oven preheated to 350°F, bake for 25–30 minutes, or until browned, turning every 10 minutes or so.

- Allow the seeds to cool before serving or storing.

Add a handful of these roasted pumpkin seeds to your favorite snack mix or sprinkle them on top of your favorite salad to boost the iron content of either dish. They also make for a pretty garnish.

Spicy Pumpkin Seeds: For a spicy, smoky flavor, add ¼ teaspoon of dried chipotle chiles to the mixture. You can also get this effect by adding 1 teaspoon of smoked paprika to the seeds. Simply toss it in with the other dried spices and olive oil, then roast as directed.

Drizzling Oil onto Seeds

Spread Out the Seeds

- Drizzle the olive oil on the seeds using a teaspoon.

- Alternatively, use a pump and simply spray the seeds until you see that they are well coated.

- Make sure the seeds are well spread out on the cookie sheet so that they roast evenly.

- To stir, take a spatula or wooden spoon to the seeds as they're roasting and try to turn as many of them over as possible.

STRAWBERRIES & BALSAMIC SAUCE

A balsamic reduction is reminiscent of chocolate syrup in this fresh fruit snack

Chocolate and strawberries is one of those age-old combinations that never fails to please. This balsamic vinegar–based sauce evokes the sweet sharpness of chocolate but with an aromatic hint that can't be found in cocoa.

Balsamic vinegar is an aged vinegar originally from Italy that, being made from grapes, is packed with antioxidants known to fight cell damage and boost the immune system. It also has antiviral and antibacterial properties, which make it a natural preservative when added to other foods.

Balsamic vinegar has also been shown to suppress people's appetites, so using it in a vinaigrette on salads can help make a salad more filling. *Yield: 1*

Ingredients

3 tablespoons balsamic vinegar

3 tablespoons sugar

10 strawberries, stems removed and quartered

Strawberries & Balsamic Sauce

- In a saucepan over low heat, combine the balsamic vinegar and sugar, stirring frequently.

- Once the sugar has dissolved and the vinegar has thickened, remove it from the heat and drizzle it over the strawberries.

Calories 230, **Fat** (g) 0, **Carbohydrates** (g) 59, **Protein** (g) 1, **Fiber** (g) 2, **Saturated Fat** (g) 0, **Cholesterol** (mg) 0, **Sodium** (mg) 16

Melon & Balsamic: Serve this balsamic-based sauce with other fresh fruits, such as cantaloupe or watermelon. Prepare the sauce as is described below, then drizzle it over the melon. Toss in a few leaves of fresh mint for color and a refreshing punch.

Angel Food Cake with Balsamic-tossed Strawberries: Turn your snack into a light yet lush-tasting dessert. Toss a handful of cut strawberries in the balsamic sauce described below, then spoon them over a slice of light-as air angel food cake.

Preparing Strawberries

- Begin by choosing ripe strawberries that are bright red in color.

- Throw away any soft or brown strawberries.

- Wash the strawberries by running them under cold water.

- Slice the caps off with a sharp paring knife.

Combining Sugar and Vinegar

- Heat the vinegar over low heat to avoid burning it.

- Using a wooden spoon, stir the vinegar as you add the sugar. Keep stirring until the sugar dissolves.

- You'll know the sauce has reduced enough when it has a syrupy consistency.

- Test this by dipping your spoon in the sauce and seeing the speed at which the excess sauce drips off. It should be slow and thick.

DEVILED EGGS
This classic party food is a great snack, even for a party of one

There are endless possibilities for how to dress up your deviled egg. Plain deviled eggs are delicious, but an extra topping of horseradish or anchovies, red bell peppers, sliced black olives, or simple fresh chives transforms the eggs from a snack to an "amuse-bouche," a little treat to entertain your taste buds. Sure, these are great to make for parties, but indulging in them at home can be a quick and easy way to treat yourself.

Take a couple in a container with a side of potato salad and a serving of fresh fruit out to your favorite park bench for the perfect picnic lunch for one.
Yield: 2 servings

Ingredients

6 hard-boiled eggs, shelled and chilled

2 tablespoons low-fat mayonnaise

1 tablespoon Worcestershire sauce

1 tablespoon red wine vinegar

Sea salt and freshly ground pepper, to taste

$1/2$ teaspoon paprika

Calories 211, **Fat** (g) 15, **Carbohydrates** (g) 4, **Protein** (g) 13, **Fiber** (g) 0, **Saturated Fat** (g) 4, **Cholesterol** (mg) 424, **Sodium** (mg) 469

Deviled Eggs

- Cut the chilled eggs in half lengthwise and scoop out the yolks.

- In a mixing bowl, mash the yolks with a fork. Mix in the mayonnaise, Worcestershire sauce, vinegar, and salt and pepper.

- Spoon the yolk mixture into the egg white halves, and finish with a sprinkle of paprika to garnish.

French Deviled Eggs: As an homage to the classic French salad of steamed asparagus and soft-boiled quail eggs, chop up a couple asparagus tips into inch-long pieces. Sauté them for a few minutes until they are tender. Let them cool a little, then nestle each piece onto the top of a finished deviled egg.

Deviled Eggs with Anchovies: Prepare your deviled eggs as described below, except add 1 tablespoon of minced canned anchovies to the egg mixture. Because anchovies are so salty, you can also omit the sea salt from the recipe.

Spooning Out Yolks

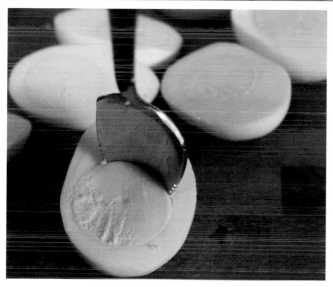

- Halve your eggs with a sharp knife.

- If your eggs are boiled just right, the yolks should pop out with the gentle nudging of a spoon.

- Use the spoon to scrape out any leftover yellow bits.

Mashing Yolks

- Mash your yolks using a fork or a potato masher.

- Break them up slightly by themselves.

- Then add the other ingredients and mash everything together until well combined.

BRUSSELS SPROUTS

These adorable mini cabbages make the perfect side to any meat

Brussels sprouts are a food we may have been averse to as children, but probably only because they weren't prepared like this. These sprouts turn out lightly browned and crisped on the outside and tender on the inside. They go well with most meats and heavier fish dishes.

Brussels sprouts, like other cruciferous vegetables, contain special sulfur-releasing phytonutrients that can help prevent cancer. They're also high in fiber and vitamin C.

We've suggested roasting the brussels sprouts for this recipe, which imparts a light crisp to the outer leaves, while ensuring the inside stays warm and tender. Halving the sprouts will allow them to cook more quickly and evenly than keeping them whole.

Yield: 4

Ingredients

1 pound brussels sprouts, halved

4 cloves garlic, minced

6 shallots, chopped

3 tablespoons olive oil

2 tablespoons grated Parmesan cheese

Sea salt and freshly ground pepper, to taste

Brussels Sprouts

- In a large bowl, toss all the ingredients together, then spread out the brussels sprouts in a roasting pan.

- In an oven preheated to 400°F, roast for 45 minutes or until brussels sprouts begin to brown.

- They're done when they're slightly crispy on the outside and tender on the inside.

Calories 162, **Fat** (g) 11, **Carbohydrates** (g) 13, **Protein** (g) 6, **Fiber** (g) 4, **Saturated Fat** (g) 2, **Cholesterol** (mg) 2, **Sodium** (mg) 168

• • • • RECIPE VARIATIONS • • • •

Citrusy Brussels Sprouts: Add a squeeze of lemon to this side dish to brighten the flavors. Prepare the sprouts as described below, but squeeze the juice of ½ a freshly squeezed lemon onto the sprouts before tossing them with the other ingredients.

Romano Brussels Sprouts: Parmesan isn't the only aged Italian cheese out there. Pecorino Romano is a sharp cheese made from sheep's milk. Instead of Parmesan cheese, add 2 tablespoons of freshly grated aged Pecorino Romano to this side dish. Rather than using a cheese grater, you can also try shaving curls of the cheese with a vegetable peeler.

Tossing Ingredients

- Toss the ingredients with salad tongs or with your hands.
- Make sure every sprout gets well coated.

Roasting the Sprouts

- While the brussels sprouts are roasting, you'll want to turn them at least once to make sure they cook evenly.
- Open the oven door and, using a spatula, quickly stir the sprouts.
- Close the oven as quickly as possible so as not to let too much heat escape.

SIDES

211

BAKED SWEET POTATO FRIES
These tasty fries will make you forget all about the deep-fryer

Thanksgiving isn't the only time of year to enjoy sweet potatoes. These bright orange root vegetables are packed with nutrients and taste delicious, so be sure to incorporate them into meals year-round. This recipe for baked sweet potato fries turns out crispy strips that are soft and chewy on the inside. You'll have a hard time believing these fries are baked.

Like many orange foods, sweet potatoes are an excellent source of beta-carotene, an important antioxidant that, along with vitamin C, can help reduce inflammation and prevent illnesses like heart disease and cancer. Sweet potatoes also contain fiber, vitamin B$_6$, potassium, and iron to help boost energy and promote both cardiovascular and digestive health.

Yield: 2 servings

Ingredients

2 large sweet potatoes, peeled and cut into thick strips

1 tablespoon olive oil

$^1/_4$ teaspoon cayenne pepper

Sea salt and freshly ground pepper, to taste

Calories 171, **Fat** (g) 7, **Carbohydrates** (g) 26, **Protein** (g) 2, **Fiber** (g) 4, **Saturated Fat** (g) 1, **Cholesterol** (mg) 0, **Sodium** (mg) 304

Baked Sweet Potato Fries

- In a large bowl, combine the potatoes, oil, and seasoning.

- Toss well to coat every strip.

- Place the potato strips on a baking sheet and, in an oven preheated to 400°F, bake the potatoes for 25–30 minutes.

- Allow the fries to cool a bit before serving.

Baked Potato Fries: This recipe also works with regular potatoes. Prepare the potatoes as described below, except use 2 large russet or Yukon Gold potatoes. Season your "fries" simply with just a pinch of sea salt and black pepper.

Italian Sweet Potato Fries: Change up the seasonings to achieve a Mediterranean effect. Prepare your baked fries as described below, except season them with pinches of sea salt, dried oregano, sweet paprika, dried basil, and garlic powder.

Slicing the Potatoes

- You can cut the sweet potatoes into thick strips or thin, depending on your preference.

- The important thing is to cut them into uniform strips so that they cook evenly.

- Leave the skins on for extra nutrients and a heartier texture.

Baking the Potatoes

- Line up the sweet potato strips in even rows on the baking sheet. This will make it easier to turn them.

- Using tongs or a spatula, turn the strips once, about halfway through the baking time, so that they crisp all over.

SIDES

ROASTED BROCCOLI
It doesn't take much to roast fresh broccoli florets to perfection

Your mother may have admonished you for not eating all your broccoli, but that was before you discovered how delicious it could be.

This simple recipe for roasted broccoli calls only for olive oil, salt, black pepper, and fresh parsley. Buy fresh and, if possible, locally farmed broccoli for this recipe and it definitely won't need anything else.

Like other cruciferous vegetables, broccoli has been shown to help protect against a slew of different cancers and promote digestive health. Consuming broccoli and other crucifers can also help fight free radicals in the body, which can otherwise damage the body's cells.

Yield: 1

Ingredients

$^1/_2$ pound broccoli, chopped into florets

1 tablespoon olive oil

Sea salt and freshly ground pepper, to taste

$^1/_4$ cup finely chopped fresh parsley

Calories 251, **Fat** (g) 15, **Carbohydrates** (g) 24, **Protein** (g) 14,
Fiber (g) 14, **Saturated Fat** (g) 2, **Cholesterol** (mg) 0,
Sodium (mg) 542

Roasted Broccoli

- In a large bowl, toss together the broccoli, oil, and salt and pepper.

- Spread out the broccoli in a roasting pan and, in an oven preheated to 400°F, roast it for 15 minutes or until the desired tenderness is achieved.

- Remove the broccoli from the oven and toss it with the parsley before serving.

GREEN ● LIGHT

Boiling broccoli can kill off most of its flavor and result in it taking on a dull green color. But because it's such a hearty vegetable, it can stand up to being roasted, which allows it to get browned slightly on the outside while staying tender on the inside.

• • • • RECIPE VARIATION • • • •

Roasted Broccoli Rabe: Broccoli Rabe is a green leafy vegetable that is in the same family as a turnip, but most closely resembles broccoli. Prepare as described below, except, it being more delicate than broccoli, you'll likely only need to roast it 8–10 minutes.

Tossing the Broccoli

- Toss the broccoli with the salt, pepper, and olive oil using salad tongs.

- Add the parsley afterward for a fresh, peppery flavor.

Roasting Broccoli

- People often throw away the stalks, but don't let these go to waste!

- The stalks are also good to eat and, when peeled and cubed, are attractive among the bright green florets.

SIDES

215

ALMOND RICE

A subtle hint of almonds turns plain brown rice into an aromatic side dish

Almonds impart nutty aromatics and a protein boost to this side dish. For this recipe, you can use store-bought almond slivers. But if you're so inclined, it's easy to make your own.

Start by blanching the almonds, then all you have to do is slip off the skins and chop them up. Instead of attempting perfect slivers like you get at the store, you're better off

roughly chopping the almonds. Place them in a pile on a cutting board and rock a sharp chef's knife back and forth over the nuts. As they scatter, gather them and continue to chop. *Yield: 6 servings*

Ingredients

1 tablespoon olive oil

¹/₂ cup almond slivers

2 cups brown rice, uncooked

1¹/₂ cups chicken or vegetable stock

Sea salt and freshly ground pepper, to taste

2 tablespoons finely chopped fresh chives

Calories 299, **Fat** (g) 7, **Carbohydrates** (g) 51, **Protein** (g) 7, **Fiber** (g) 3, **Saturated Fat** (g) 1, **Cholesterol** (mg) 0, **Sodium** (mg) 168

Almond Rice

- Spray a saucepan with oil and, over medium-high heat, add almonds. Pan-roast a couple minutes, until slightly browned.

- Spray the saucepan with a little more oil and add rice. Cook for a minute or two, until the rice starts to brown.

- Pour the stock over top, and add salt and pepper, stirring well. Cover the pot and bring to a boil. Once bubbles start to appear, reduce the heat to low and allow rice to simmer for about 20 minutes.

- Uncover the pot and stir in chives.

Almond & Raisin Rice: Add a touch of sweetness and another dimension of texture to this dish by adding ½ cup of raisins to it. Prepare it as described below, then add the raisins at the end, when you stir in the chives.

Pine Nut Rice: Change the flavors in this dish by using toasted pine nuts instead of almond slivers. Spray ½ cup pine nuts with olive oil on a baking tin, then toast them in the oven at 250 for 10 minutes. Prepare the rice as described below, except substitute the almonds for the pine nuts.

Blanching Almonds

Pan-roasting Almonds

- Start by blanching the almonds. Place raw almonds in a bowl, and pour boiling water over them, just enough to cover the almonds.

- Let them sit in the hot water for 1 minute, then drain and rinse them under cold water in a colander.

- Don't let the almonds stay in the hot water longer than 1 minute or they'll get soft.

- Transfer the almonds to a large, flat surface covered in paper towels. Now you can easily slip the skins off the almonds.

- You don't need much moisture to pan-roast the almonds. Spraying the pan with oil should be enough.

- If you have a nonstick pan, you can dry roast the almonds.

SIDES

SIMPLE POLENTA

With polenta, the possibilities are endless—start simple or get creative

Polenta can be made in so many ways that there is very likely an all-polenta cookbook out there. You can make polenta soft and creamy, or firm like a cake. And speaking of cake, you can make polenta into desserts that resemble sponge cakes.

You can make polenta simply or add vegetables, meats, fruits, cheese, fresh herbs, or dried spices to it. It may just be one of the most versatile grains out there. And, because of its long shelf life, you can always keep a box of it in the pantry for last-minute side dishes or to impress drop-in guests.
Yield: 2 servings

Ingredients

1 cup coarsely ground yellow polenta

1 teaspoon sea salt

3 cups water

1 tablespoon olive oil

Calories 312, **Fat** (g) 8, **Carbohydrates** (g) 54, **Protein** (g) 6, **Fiber** (g) 5, **Saturated Fat** (g) 1, **Cholesterol** (mg) 0, **Sodium** (mg) 1165

Simple Polenta

- In a bowl, combine the polenta, salt, and 1 cup of the water, mixing well.

- In a saucepan over medium heat, bring the rest of the water to a boil.

- Pour the polenta mixture into the boiling water, stirring constantly until it returns to a boil.

- Reduce the heat to low, and add the olive oil to the polenta mixture.

- Continue stirring intermittently for about 20–30 minutes, or until the desired consistency has been achieved.

Firm Polenta: For this recipe, the polenta is soft, served at a grits consistency. For a firm polenta, take the creamy polenta mixture and transfer it to an oiled loaf pan. Cover it and chill it overnight. In the morning, turn the polenta out, slice it, and grill it or toast it in the oven.

Spicy Polenta: Kick up your polenta with a bit of heat. Prepare the polenta as is described below, except stir 1 teaspoon minced Serrano chiles into the cornmeal mixture. Then, set it in an oiled loaf pan as described at left to be chilled overnight. Slice the firm polenta into inch-thick slabs and toast or grill them.

Mixing Cornmeal

- When adding the cornmeal to the cold water, do so gradually.

- Using a whisk, mix it well, so that everything is properly incorporated.

- When you add the corn-meal mixture to the boiling water, again, do it a little at a time, stirring continuously.

Stirring Polenta in Saucepan

- The consistency of polenta should be like that of grits or an oatmeal.

- You can always thin it with water if it becomes too thick.

SIDES

POTATO & GREEN BEAN SALAD
Add some color to your potato salad with crisp fresh green beans

Potato salad is a picnic mainstay. For this recipe, the potatoes are roasted instead of boiled, and the delicate skins are left on to seal in the flavors and nutrients. The salad can be served lukewarm or at room temperature, or you can choose to chill it overnight.

We've recommended using red and white new potatoes, but if you can find blue potatoes as well, the salad will look even prettier—and it becomes the perfect red-white-and-blue potato salad for the Fourth of July!

Blue potatoes not only look pretty but, like other brightly colored foods, contain many important nutrients. As well, blue potatoes can have up to 90 times more antioxidants than white ones.

Yield: 2

Ingredients

1 pound red and white new potatoes, quartered with skins on

Sea salt and freshly ground pepper, to taste

1 tablespoon olive oil

¹/₂ pound green beans

3 tablespoons low-fat mayonnaise

¹/₄ cup finely chopped fresh chives

¹/₂ teaspoon paprika

¹/₂ teaspoon cayenne pepper

Calories 341, **Fat** (g) 14, **Carbohydrates** (g) 49, **Protein** (g) 7, **Fiber** (g) 7, **Saturated Fat** (g) 2, **Cholesterol** (mg) 0, **Sodium** (mg) 401

Potato and Green Bean Salad

- In a bowl, combine potatoes and salt and pepper and toss with oil.

- Place potatoes in a roasting pan and, in an oven preheated to 400°F, roast for 25–30 minutes, turning once.

- About 15–20 minutes into the cooking time, add the green beans to the pan.

- Remove potatoes and green beans. Let cool for at least 10 minutes.

- Toss potatoes and green beans with the mayonnaise, chives, paprika, and cayenne pepper.

Cheesy Potato Salad : Take a wedge of Parmesan or Romano cheese and, using a potato peeler, shave several curls of cheese on top of each serving. Alternatively, toss the Parmesan in with the salad. You can also use a cheese grater for this task.

Potato & Beet Salad: Roasted red beets add a splash of color and a shot of fiber and iron to this salad. Prepare the salad as described below, except add 1 cup cubed roasted beets to the mix when you toss it.

Tossing Potatoes with Oil

Potatoes in the Roasting Pan

- To prep the potatoes, wash them, then scrape off any blemished areas.

- Quarter the potatoes, but leave the skins on to maximize the nutrient content of the salad.

- Toss the potatoes using salad tongs.

- New potatoes don't take too long to cook. Monitor them closely to make sure they do not burn.

- The potatoes should be slightly browned, but not charred.

- The green beans should retain their bright green color, and be cooked al dente.

SIDES

221

BANANA LOAF

Enjoy this moist and delicious loaf for dessert or try a slice for breakfast

What to do with bananas that have gotten overripe? Mash them up to make this tasty banana loaf. Once you notice your bananas turning brown, you can toss them in the freezer and make this loaf at a later date.

Everyone knows bananas are high in potassium, but they also are rich in vitamin B$_6$, which is important to the health of nearly every major system in the body.

This light dessert can make for a tasty snack or even part of a delicious breakfast… and how often can you have dessert for breakfast without feeling guilty about it? We love serving it warm with a tiny pat of butter.

Yield: 8

Ingredients

¹/₂ cup plain low-fat yogurt

1 egg plus 1 egg white

¹/₂ cup sugar

1 teaspoon vanilla

1¹/₂ cups all-purpose flour

¹/₂ cup whole wheat flour

¹/₂ teaspoon baking powder

³/₄ teaspoon baking soda

¹/₂ teaspoon salt

¹/₄ teaspoon nutmeg

2 overripe bananas

2 teaspoons vinegar

¹/₄ cup nonfat milk

Calories 146, **Fat** (g) 1, **Carbohydrates** (g) 31, **Protein** (g) 4, **Fiber** (g) 1, **Saturated Fat** (g) 0, **Cholesterol** (mg) 18, **Sodium** (mg) 191

Banana Loaf

- In a mixing bowl, combine the yogurt, eggs, sugar, and vanilla, mixing until creamy. In another bowl, sift together the flours, baking powder, baking soda, salt, and nutmeg.

- Mix mashed bananas with wet ingredients. Prep vinegar and milk in another bowl. Combine all ingredients in one bowl and mix until batter is smooth.

- Pour batter into greased baking tin and, in an oven heated to 350°F, bake 25–30 minutes or until cooked through.

- Remove loaf and unmold.

Nutty Banana Bread: Take 1 cup of raw walnuts and toss them into a dry pan over medium heat. Pan-roast the walnuts for a few minutes, until they brown a little. Once they've cooled a bit, chop them up on a cutting board with a sharp chef's knife, then add them to the batter before baking the loaf.

Chocolate Chip Banana Bread: Add a touch of sweetness to this recipe by tossing mini semisweet chocolate chips into the batter. Prepare batter as described below, then take 1 cup of chocolate chips and fold them into the batter before pouring it into the baking tin.

Mashing Bananas and Prepping Ingredients

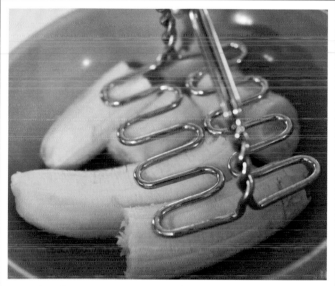

- In a bowl, mash the bananas using a fork or potato masher.

- Add the mashed bananas to the wet mixture, mixing well.

- In a third bowl, stir the vinegar into the milk until it curdles.

- Combine all the ingredients and mix until batter is smooth.

Pouring Batter into Pan

- Spray a rectangular baking tin with vegetable oil.

- Pour batter into the tin and bake.

- After baked, allow loaf to rest 5 minutes before unmolding. Be gentle in the unmolding process, as the loaf may crack.

DESSERTS

APPLE CRISP

Sweet and tangy and crunchy all at once, this dessert is best enjoyed warm

The crunch of the topping and the moistness of the sweet and tart baked apples in this dessert make for the perfect after dinner treat.

You can use any type of apple for this dessert, from tart Granny Smiths to sweet Fujis. But the dish is most interesting with a mix of different types of apples: some sweeter, others more tart. Why not turn dessert into a fun day out by picking your own apples for the crisp? Head out to an orchard that offers apple picking and you can be sure to have the freshest dessert ever.

This apple crisp is best served warm with a side of nonfat vanilla frozen yogurt. *Yield: 4*

Ingredients

1 pound apples, peeled and sliced

1 tablespoon cornstarch

1 teaspoon lemon juice

1 teaspoon grated fresh lemon zest

1/4 cup sugar

1/4 cup whole wheat flour

Pinch of cinnamon

Pinch of nutmeg

Pinch of salt

1/4 cup plain nonfat yogurt

1/4 cup quick rolled oats

Calories 156, **Fat** (g) 1, **Carbohydrates** (g) 37, **Protein** (g) 3, **Fiber** (g) 3, **Saturated Fat** (g) 0, **Cholesterol** (mg) 0, **Sodium** (mg) 129

Apple Crisp

- In a bowl, toss the apples with the cornstarch, lemon juice, and lemon zest.

- Place the apples in a lightly oiled square baking dish.

- In another bowl, combine the sugar, flour, and seasonings, mixing well.

- Add the yogurt and oats, stirring until a crumbly texture is achieved.

- Spoon the mixture over the apples and, in an oven preheated to 350°F, bake for 45 minutes or until the top begins to brown.

Apple Cranberry Crisp: Add 1 cup of raisins or dried cranberries to the apple, lemon, and cornstarch mixture. In addition to a burst of flavor and a chewy texture, each adds a concentrated dose of antioxidants, which are important to fighting disease and strengthening the immune system, to the dessert. Raisins also boast the trace mineral boron, an important nutrient for bone health.

Blueberry Apple Crisp: Another way to add something special to this traditional apple crisp recipe is to toss fresh blueberries into the mix. Add 1 cup fresh whole blueberries to the apples in the baking tin before pouring the oat mixture over top.

Preparing the Apples

- To prep the apples, peel them, core them, and slice them into wedges.

- It's a good idea to add the lemon juice to the freshly peeled and sliced apples immediately to prevent them from turning brown.

Spooning Oat Mixture onto Apples

- Be sure to spread the oat mixture evenly over the apples in the baking tin.

- The mixture should end up being about ¾ of an inch thick, so if you find yourself with not enough, you may need a smaller baking tin.

DESSERTS

POACHED PEARS

Poaching fresh, ripe fruit in its own juices requires no extra sugar

Work with ripe—but not overripe—pears for this simple dessert. We recommend leaving the skins on, but you can peel the pears if you prefer.

Yield: 2

Ingredients

Juice of ¹/₂ lemon

¹/₄ teaspoon cinnamon

¹/₄ teaspoon nutmeg

¹/₂ cup apple cider

¹/₄ cup water

2 pears, peeled, halved, and cored

Calories 122, **Fat** (g) 0, **Carbohydrates** (g) 32, **Protein** (g) 1, **Fiber** (g) 5, **Saturated Fat** (g) 0, **Cholesterol** (mg) 0, **Sodium** (mg) 7

Poached Pears

- In a saucepan over medium heat, combine the lemon juice, cinnamon, nutmeg, apple cider, and water.

- Stir well. Add the pears and cover.

- Simmer for 15–20 minutes, turning pears intermittently.

- Remove the pears from the saucepan and, over high heat, bring the remaining liquid to a boil. Boil for about 15 minutes or until it has reduced to a syrupy consistency.

- Drizzle syrup over the pears and serve.

Variation 1: To add an extra kick to this dessert, use a dry or off-dry sparkling wine instead of apple cider. As the pears cook, the alcohol will burn off, but it will suffuse the dessert with a lovely aromatic essence.

Variation 2: Serve this dish with a dollop of whipped low-fat cream cheese in each pear half. Either start with whipped cream cheese or whip regular low-fat cream cheese yourself. Use a teaspoon to plop a dollop of the cream cheese into the center of each pear half.

Pears Cooking

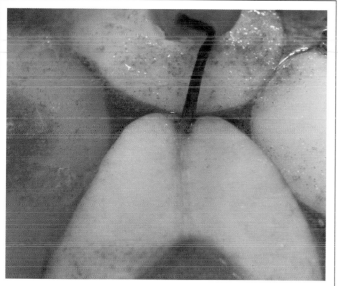

Drizzling Syrup

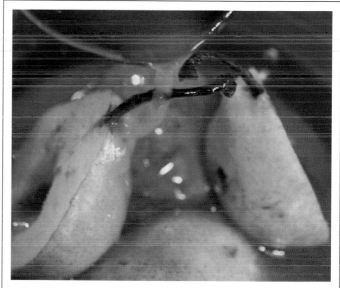

- The finished pears should be firm enough that they keep their shape, but able to slice into with a spoon.

- To check on the doneness of your pears, use a fork to pierce one of them.

- If you feel any resistance at all, leave them cooking a little longer.

- But don't overcook! Remember, they will continue to cook in their own juices for a minute or so after they are removed from the saucepan.

- To make sure your syrup has the right consistency, dip a spoon inside and, when you pull it out, it should drip into a steady stream.

- Each pear only needs about 1 tablespoon of syrup drizzled over top.

DESSERTS

STRAWBERRY RHUBARB PARFAIT

This perfect combination of summer fruits brings sweet and tart together beautifully

Strawberries and rhubarb are one of those quintessentially summery fruit combinations. You can find them in pies, in cakes, and in this light and delicious parfait. The rhubarb, a relative of buckwheat, has its super-sour taste softened and sweetened by ripe strawberries. Both fruits are good sources of fiber and vitamin C, as well as a slew of other essential nutrients. But be careful with rhubarb—while the stalks make for delightfully tangy desserts, the leaves are toxic, whether cooked or raw.

We suggest assembling this parfait once the stewed rhubarb has cooled, but don't let it cool completely—slightly warm rhubarb with ice cold ice cream is delicious. *Yield: 2*

Ingredients

¹/₂ pound rhubarb stalks, chopped

¹/₂ pound strawberries, chopped

¹/₂ cup sugar

1 cup low-fat vanilla ice cream or frozen yogurt

Calories 351, **Fat** (g) 4, **Carbohydrates** (g) 77, **Protein** (g) 4, **Fiber** (g) 3, **Saturated Fat** (g) 2, **Cholesterol** (mg) 36, **Sodium** (mg) 53

Strawberry Rhubarb Parfait

- In a bowl, toss the rhubarb and strawberries together with the sugar.

- In a saucepan over medium-low heat, stew the fruit, stirring intermittently, for 10–12 minutes, or until it starts to break down.

- Remove the mixture from the heat and allow it to cool for 10–15 minutes.

- Assemble parfait and serve immediately.

Minty Strawberry Rhubarb Parfait: A few leaves of fresh mint will bring this dessert to life. Remove the leaves from the mint stem and chop finely, saving a few full leaves for a garnish. Toss the chopped leaves into the fruit mixture about 5 minutes before it's done cooking. When you're layering the fruit and ice cream, place the whole leaves on top as a garnish.

Using Frozen Fruit: Chop the rhubarb into inch-long pieces, removing extra fibers. Place it on a cookie sheet and freeze overnight. Seal the frozen rhubarb pieces into an airtight container. Place it in the coldest part of the freezer for up to nine months. For strawberries, clear and cut stems off them, and follow the same procedure. Date your container so that you know how long to keep the fruit.

Prepping Fruit

- Before stewing the fruit, be sure that all the leaves and the ends of the stems have been removed from the rhubarb.

- The leaves, in particular, should be discarded, as they are poisonous.

- Once the fruit starts to stew, cook it until it starts to break down.

Assembling Parfait

- Layer some of the ice cream or frozen yogurt with some of the fruit mixture in a tall glass.

- Repeat until you have 3–4 layers. Serve immediately.

DESSERTS

LEMON LOAF

Real citrus flavors and aromas permeate this light yet lush lemon loaf

Real lemons and tangy yogurt go into this simple loaf. Try using Splenda or some other artificial sweetener instead of sugar. They can almost always be substituted one-to-one.

Lemons are, of course, an excellent source of vitamin C. But did you know that they are also high in potassium, which can help control high blood pressure? Lemons also contain fiber

and compounds called limonins, which have been shown to fight all sorts of cancers.

This tangy, not too sweet dessert is delicious on its own, but we've suggested preparing it with a simple glaze to make it extra special.

Yield: 8–10 servings

Ingredients

1 cup plain nonfat Greek yogurt

2 cups Splenda, divided

2 eggs plus 2 egg whites

2 teaspoons lemon zest

1/4 teaspoon vanilla extract

1 1/2 cups all-purpose flour

2 teaspoons baking powder

1/2 teaspoon salt

1/4 cup nonfat milk

Juice of 1 lemon

1/4 cup vegetable oil

Calories 307, **Fat** (g) 7, **Carbohydrates** (g) 57, **Protein** (g) 6, **Fiber** (g) 1, **Saturated Fat** (g) 1, **Cholesterol** (mg) 43, **Sodium** (mg) 261

Lemon Loaf

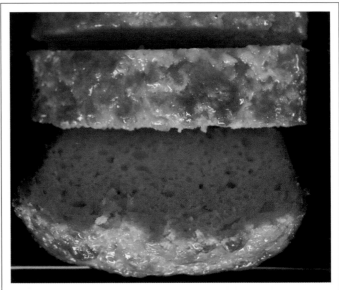

- In a mixing bowl, cream together yogurt, oil, half of the Splenda, eggs, lemon zest, and vanilla extract.

- In a separate bowl, combine flour, baking powder, and salt. Little by little, add dry mixture to wet, mixing well. Then fold in milk.

- In a separate bowl, combine lemon juice with the rest of the Splenda. Mix well until glaze achieves a syrupy consistency.

- Pour batter into a greased and floured baking tin. In a 350°F preheated oven, bake 50 minutes. When done, pour glaze over top.

Because you'll be zesting the lemon, be sure to wash it thoroughly. Look for organic lemons, which are free of pesticides that can sit on the rinds. You should also pick lemons with a thinner skin, as thicker-skinned lemons have less flesh and juice.

•••• RECIPE VARIATION ••••

Lemon & Poppy Seed Loaf: Prepare the lemon loaf as described below, except fold ½ cup poppy seeds into the batter. Poppy seeds are a source of omega-6 fatty acids, which are important to cardiovascular health. They are also known to have anti-inflammatory properties . . . just don't take a drug test after consuming them. Remember, they're what opium is made from!

Adding the Dry Mixture to Wet

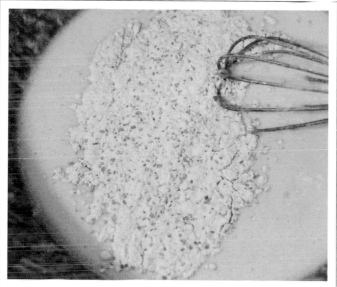

- Add the dry mixture to the wet little by little to ensure that they are well incorporated.

- You can mix the two together by hand, using a whisk , or in an electric mixer on low.

Pouring Batter into the Baking Tin

- Lightly oil your baking tin by spraying it with vegetable oil.

- Alternatively, you can take a paper towel, dab it with oil, and rub it along the insides of the tin.

- Dust the baking tin with a little flour before pouring in the batter.

DESSERTS

CHOCOLATE CHIP COOKIES

Cut the butter in half for a lighter, crispier chocolate chip cookie

Chocolate chip cookies are a weakness for many of us. But why should they be? By using half the butter called for in other recipes, you can make a lighter, crispier chocolate chip cookie with significantly fewer calories.

We also cut the sugar in this recipe—not only to cut the calories, but because sweeter isn't always better when it comes to dessert. Why do you think chocolate chip cookies are best washed down with a cold glass of milk? It's because

your palate needs something to cut the sweetness and milk is the best way to do so. You won't miss out on sweetness with these tasty cookies. And you can still wash them down with a cold glass of milk!

Yield: 12

Ingredients

1 cup all-purpose flour

1/2 teaspoon baking soda

1/2 teaspoon salt

3 tablespoons unsalted butter, softened

1/4 cup brown sugar

1 egg white

1 teaspoon vanilla extract

1/2 cup semisweet chocolate chips

Chocolate Chip Cookies

- In a mixing bowl, combine the flour, baking soda, and salt.

- In a separate bowl, cream together the butter, brown sugar, egg, and vanilla until smooth. Add chocolate chips.

- On a nonstick cookie sheet, spoon out dough. In a 325°F preheated oven, bake 10–12 minutes.

- Allow cookies to cool before serving.

Calories 102, **Fat** (g) 3, **Carbohydrates** (g) 17, **Protein** (g) 2, **Fiber** (g) 1, **Saturated Fat** (g) 2, **Cholesterol** (mg) 3, **Sodium** (mg) 157

Creaming Together Ingredients

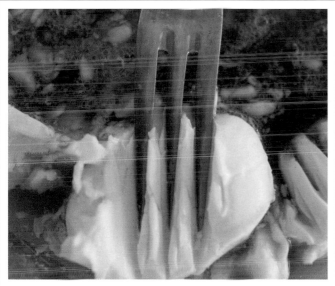

- Little by little, add the dry mixture to the wet mixture.

- Fold in the chocolate chips until well spread out throughout the batter.

- Do not over handle the batter at this point as you can damage the chocolate chips and stress out the dough.

Spooning Out Dough

- On a nonstick cookie sheet, spoon 2-tablespoon-sized portions of the batter out about 2 inches apart.

- Do not spoon too closely together, or else cookies might merge together when baking.

DESSERTS

MANUFACTURERS & WEB SITES

Find important information about counting calories online and offline

When it comes to losing weight or maintaining your weight, you don't have to go it alone. A number of resources both online and offline can help you track your daily caloric intake, as well as offer tips and advice on how best to begin a weight management program.

Should you be a beginner in the kitchen, you'll need to stock up on some basic cookware. You don't need to have state-of-the-art kitchen equipment. If you're just starting out, there are certain basics every home cook needs: a good skillet, a good saucepan, and a good baking dish. The rest, as they say, is gravy.

Finally, if you're embarking on a weight loss or weight management plan, you'll need basic health and nutrition

advice. Consulting a registered nutritionist can be invaluable. There are also numerous Web sites that can be great sources of information and advice.

The Calorie Counter
http://thecaloriecounter.com
The Calorie Counter helps you calculate your daily caloric intake by allowing you to easily enter the foods you've eaten to get a daily total.

H. F. Coors Company
www.hfcoorsdinnerware.com
H. F. Coors Company is located in Tucson, Arizona, and has a Web site featuring a collection of fine dinnerware, including plates, bowls, and platters made right here in the United States.

Lose It!
www.freshapps.com/lose-it
Visit the site to download Lose It!, an iPhone application that works as a calorie counter you can carry with you everywhere. Enter the foods you've eaten and the physical activities you've undertaken for an accurate daily caloric calculation.

The Nutritionists Directory
http://nutritionists.healthprofs.com
This online directory helps you find a registered nutritionist in your area. Nutritionists are great sources of information and advice if you're looking to manage your weight.

Nutrition.gov
www.nutrition.gov
Nutrition.gov provides information on health and nutrition from the federal government, including science-based dietary facts and professional advice for men and women of all ages, as well as children.

The Kitchen Store
www.thekitchenstore.com
The name says it all! Get everything you need to stock your kitchen at this online destination for cookware, bakeware, and all the necessary accoutrements for your kitchen.

Overeaters Anonymous
www.oa.org
If weight loss is more than a challenge for you, you don't have to go it alone. Overeaters Anonymous offers a twelve-step program, as well as the support of others who have walked in your shoes.

Sur La Table
www.surlatable.com
Sur La Table is an online store for everything kitchen-related. Buy cookware, dishware, and those handy spray pumps for olive oil at this popular store's Web site.

Weight-control Information Network (WIN)
http://win.niddk.nih.gov
The Weight-control Information Network (WIN) is an information service established to provide up-to-date science-based information on obesity, weight control, physical activity, and related nutrition issues.

Weight Watchers
www.weightwatchers.com
The iconic weight loss program has been around for 40 years and still works better than any fad diet out there. Based on eating nutritious foods in the correct portions, Weight Watchers works.

Whole Foods Market
www.wholefoodsmarket.com
For fresh, organic, and local foods, visit your local Whole Foods Market. In many cases, the provenance of produce is listed, so you'll know how far it's traveled. The store's own organic brand is often an affordable option. Use the Web site to find a store near you.

YMCA
www.ymca.net
The YMCA features fitness centers across the country that offer affordable memberships to their gyms and diverse exercise programs, including team sports and yoga classes. Visit the Web site to find a Y near you.

ADDITIONAL RESOURCES

Subscribe to one of the following magazines for monthly news, personal stories, and advice on healthy eating and living.

Cooking Light
Its motto of "Eat Smart. Be Fit. Live Well" says it all.
www.cookinglight.com

Eating Well
This magazine focuses on tasty food that's good for you and good for the environment.
www.eatingwell.com

Fitness
Learn how to work out, manage weight, and find balance with *Fitness*.
www.fitnessmagazine.com

Health
Get science-based information on your health and your body here.
www.health.com

Men's Health
Because men also need health and nutrition advice.
www.menshealth.com

Natural Health
"Feel Good. Look Good. Do Good" is the motto here.
www.naturalhealthmag.com

Self
Tips and stories on looking and feeling your best here.
www.self.com

Shape
Learn how to exercise and eat well with this magazine.
www.shape.com

METRIC CONVERSION TABLES

Approximate U.S. Metric Equivalents

Liquid Ingredients

U.S. MEASURES	METRIC	U.S. MEASURES	METRIC
1/4 TSP.	1.23 ML	2 TBSP	29.57 ML
1/2 TSP.	2.36 ML	3 TBSP.	44.36 ML
3/4 TSP.	3.70 ML	1/4 CUP	59.15 ML
1 TSP.	4.93 ML	1/2 CUP	118.30 ML
1 1/4 TSP.	6.16 ML	1 CUP	236.59 ML
1 1/2 TSP.	7.39 ML	2 CUPS OR 1 PT.	473.18 ML
1 3/4 TSP.	8.63 Ml	3 CUPS	709.77 ML
2 TSP.	9.86 ML	4 CUPS OR 1 QT.	946.36 ML
1 TBSP.	14.79 ML	4 QTS. OR 1 GAL.	3.79 l

Dry Ingredients

U.S. MEASURES	METRIC	U.S. MEASURES		METRIC
1/16 OZ.	2 (1.8) G	2 4/5 OZ.		80 G
1/8 OZ.	3 1/2 (3.5) G	3 OZ		85 (84.9) G
1/4 OZ.	7 (7.1) G	3 1/2 OZ.		100 G
1/2 OZ.	15 (14.2) G	4 OZ.		115 (113.2) G
3/4 OZ.	21 (21.3) G	4 1/2 OZ.		125 G
7/8 OZ.	25 G	5 1/4 OZ.		150 G
1 OZ.	30 (28.3) G	8 7/8 OZ.		250 G
1 3/4 OZ.	50 G	16 OZ.	1 LB.	454 G
2 OZ.	60 (56.6) G	17 3/5 OZ.	1 LIVRE	500 G

GLOSSARY OF TERMS

Al dente: This Italian phrase translates as "to the tooth." It refers to cooking pasta, risotto, or vegetables to the point where they give a slight resistance to being chewed.

Blend: To mix ingredients together thoroughly, either by hand or using a mixer.

Boil: To bring liquid to the point where it bubbles vigorously. For water, it's 212°F.

Calorie: A unit of energy commonly used to measure how much energy can be gained from foods or expended through exercise. In popular usage, it's interchangeable with *kilocalorie*.

Cream: To mix together ingredients for cookies or cakes, such as butter and sugar, until the mixture is light, fluffy, and thoroughly blended.

Chop: To cut up into pieces. *Roughly chop* refers to cutting without aiming for a specific size.

Cube: To cut into cubes.

Dash: A measuring term that refers to a very small amount of seasoning, between 1/16 and 1/8 of a teaspoon.

Deglaze: To use a liquid—often wine—to remove the browned, caramelized bits left at the bottom of a pan after searing.

Dice: To chop into small, die-shaped pieces. (Smaller than cubes.)

Fold: To gently integrate an ingredient into a mixture, using a rubber spatula or spoon, without losing volume.

Garnish: A decorative yet edible addition to a finished dish.

Julienne: To cut food into thin strips, also called matchsticks.

Knead: To work dough by mixing, stretching, pressing, and pulling it.

Marinade: A seasoned liquid into which a meat or vegetable is placed for a specific period of time to flavor it. To *marinate* is to undergo this process.

Preheat: To heat up an oven to a predetermined temperature before cooking.

Sauté: To cook a food briefly in oil over medium-high heat, while stirring it so it cooks evenly.

Sear: To brown the surface of a food over high heat, usually with little oil or fat so a visible sear is achieved. This cooking technique is often used to seal in juices when cooking meat.

Simmer: To keep a liquid just below the boiling point. Smaller bubbles appear than if at a boil.

Skim: To remove the foamy film floating on the surface of a heated liquid with a spoon or ladle. Soups and sauces are often skimmed.

INDEX

INDEX

INDEX